HARDSHIP AND HIGH LIVING
IRISH WOMEN'S LIVES
1808 - 1923

NELLIE Ó CLÉIRIGH

Portobello Press

Portobello Press,

38 Templemore Avenue,

Rathgar,

Dublin 6.

Published in Ireland by Portobello Press 2003.

Copyright (c) Nellie Ó Cléirigh 2003

ISBN 0-9519249-1-5

Hardship and High Living: Irish Women's Lives 1808-1923

Printed and bound by Colour Books Ltd, Baldoyle Ind Est. Co. Dublin

Publisher: Niall Ó Cléirigh

Editor: Nessa O'Mahony

Cover Design: Eimear Gallagher (eimear@workworks.net)

For Cormac

Contents

Acknowledgements

I would like to express my thanks to everyone who helped in the research and writing of Hardship and High Living.

For drawing my attention to the diaries of Mary Beaufort, Selina Crampton and Cecilia Saunders-Gallagher I wish to thank Felicity O'Mahony and Jane Maxwell in the Manuscripts Department of Trinity College, Dublin. I also got much help from Eileen Cook and Monica Henchy as I did from the staff of Trinity Libraries generally.

Anne Gallagher very kindly gave me permission to quote large extracts from the diary of Cecilia Saunders Gallagher, her mother. She also provided a family background that was most useful. Permission to quote from the manuscripts MSS 4035, 4197 and 10055 has been kindly granted by the Board of Trinity College, Dublin. I am most grateful for this and for permission to reproduce the pictures of the life of Aran Islanders from their copy of Glimpses of my life on Aran by B.M. Hedderman.

Maria Luddy told me of the existence of the letters of Maria Edgeworth in the Ballytore Papers in the National Library and Marie O'Neill kindly gave me access to her paper on Maria Edgeworth which formed the background to her letters. I wish to thank them both.

Eilis Ellis drew my attention to the Commissioners of Woods Papers in the National Archives which she had used for her paper "State-Aided Emigration Schemes from Crown Estates in Ireland C. 1850. "The emigrant's letter" is based on this material. Eilis Ellis gave permission to quote from her paper for which I am very grateful.

Anne Lanigan very kindly gave me access to her research on Tipperary Workhouses undertaken for her Masters in Education. She is a teacher and qualified solicitor working in Thurles, Co. Tipperary. This research forms the basis for the chapter on the lives of Workhouse women. For information on life in other Workhouses I am indebted to Eva O'Cathaoir who told me about Fanny Taylor, Founder of the "Poor Servants of the Mother of God" Order and the involvement of these nuns with the Loughlinstown Workhouse. Sister Veronica Crowley of the Order's Convent at Ardeevin, Chapelizod, Dublin, was most helpful. Sister Marie Bernadette of the

Sisters of Charity Archives at Caritas also was a great help. Others who contributed were Sister Teresa Delaney, Sisters of Mercy Convent, Galway and Sister Agnes Gleeson, Mercy International, Baggot St., Dublin.

Veronica Rowe kindly allowed me to quote from the papers of her grandmother, Mrs Florence O'Brien, in the chapter on the lace-makers. She also allowed me to reproduce some of her photos.

Captain J.C. Gallagher very kindly lent me his copy of Memories of the Crimea by Sister Mary Aloysius after I had failed to locate a copy in any of the Libraries. Sister M. de Lourdes Fahy of the Mercy Convent, Gort, has very kindly sent me the photograph of Sister Aloysius. Sister Teresa Green of the Mercy Convent in Parker's Row, Bermondsey, London, was most helpful in giving me the drawings of the Koulali Barrack Hospital and the "Hut Hospital" in Balaclava as well as much other material. The Head House of the Mercy Order in Baggot St., Dublin allowed me access to their archives. David Murphy told me of the existence of Crimea 1854-6, the War with Russia from Contemporary Photographs by Lawrence James.

I wish to thank the staffs of the various libraries I consulted, Trinity College, The National Library, The Gilbert Library, the Royal Dublin Society and University College Dublin.

Beatrice Dixon was, as usual, generous in letting me consult her library. Karen O'Flanagan deserves a special "thank you" for ideas and encouragement.

I wish to thank Mary Purcell and the Staff of the Board of Works for locating the photo of Portumna Castle. My special thanks to Karl Magee, Archival Manager of the Adelaide and Meath Hospitals, Tallaght, Co. Dublin for getting a copy of the drawing of an operation in a Dublin drawingroom and for locating pictures of Philip Crampton. I wish to thank the Governors of the Meath Hospital for permission to reproduce these pictures.

The staff of the Irish Architectural Archive, Merrion Square, Dublin were most helpful in tracing drawings of Workhouses and permission has been given to re-produce.

Lastly I wish to thank Professor Donal McCartney for kindly writing the Foreword, Nessa O'Mahony for such a wonderful job on editing the text, and Niall for publishing the book.

4

Foreword

Nellie Ó Cléirigh's book is a valuable contribution to the social history of Ireland in the nineteenth century. More particularly it offers a variety of aspects of the lives of women in Ireland between the passing of the Act of Union in 1800 and the establishment of the Free State in the early 1920s. The high living of the fortunate few and the hardships of the multitude are portrayed through the forgotten voices of women themselves. In doing this Mrs Ó Cléirigh brings fresh manuscript material to light from the diaries of some of these women, or she exhumes their commentaries or comments about them from long out of print publications. The extensive and effective use which she makes of her source material provides her readers with a vivid insight into what life was like for the women of Ireland in that distressful century.

The gap that existed between women at the top and at the bottom of the social ladder emerges clearly in the separate chapters of this book. One is struck by the contrast between the feasts provided on the table of a Dublin surgeon and the famine fare in fishing villages of Donegal or in the soup kitchens of the midlands or in the Poor Law Workhouses of Tipperary. The events recorded might have come from worlds that were not only different, but as if they were also centuries apart. Yet the feasts and the famines were all happening in the same century and in locations that were only a carriage-ride distance from each other.

Taken together these eleven chapters illuminate the human face of Irish social history under the Union. What unfolds is a varied story of the pleasures of the few, the destitution of the many and the heroic efforts of the well-intentioned others who tried to ease the sufferings of their fellows. And against the dark social background there are also the heart-warming profiles in courage – Irish nuns contending with pestilence and war in the Crimea; a lone district nurse battling not only against superstition but also against giant Atlantic waves and storms on the Aran Islands; a 79-year-old Maria Edgeworth writing begging letters on behalf of her starving neighbours in Longford; a barely literate emigrant girl in America caring for her family back home; and the inevitable republican women jailed and ready to go on hunger-strike for their principles.

Hardship and High Living

Nellie Ó Cléirigh's earlier books on Carrickmacross and Limerick lace and her account of Valentia Island testify to a life-long interest in the lives of Irish women. Readers of this, her latest book, cannot fail to be moved by the rich vein of social history which the individual chapters reveal. I compliment her on her imaginative approach and recommend her book to all who are interested in how women coped in nineteenth century Ireland.

Donal McCartney

Professor Emeritus of Modern Irish History

University College Dublin

Introduction

The eleven 'lives' in this book have been chosen because they provide fascinating insights into the lives and social conditions of women in Ireland from 1808 until 1923. These dates cover the period from just after the Act of Union with Great Britain (in 1801) to the establishment of an independent Irish State. Through the compilation of diaries, letters and critical studies, I am attempting to convey the reality of the social restrictions, conventions and injustices plaguing Irish women during the nineteenth and early twentieth centuries.

The eleven portraits range from women in the lowest social classes to the highest, from the poorest literacy and education to the greatest. These women's lives are engaging, humorous, saddening and, most important of all, deeply telling of the times and conditions of life for Irish women.

I have taken the accounts from contemporary sources; from diaries, contemporary records and published material. They span the social spectrum from Lady Aberdeen, wife of the Viceroy, living in the Viceregal Lodge in the Phoenix Park, to the emigrant Margaret McCarthy, making a new life for herself in New York, and Ansty Cunningham, suffering the deprivations of a Tipperary Workhouse.

Three chapters, those dealing with Mary Beaufort, Selina Crampton and Cecilia Saunders Gallagher, are based on unpublished diaries held by Trinity College Dublin, and are vibrant with the immediacy of the eye witness report. The account of the emigrant's journey from Kingwilliamstown on the Cork-Kerry border to New York and Buffalo, which took place just after the Great Famine of 1847, is taken from the Commissioners of Woods Papers in the National Archives.

Details of Maria Edgeworth's efforts with the Quaker Famine relief in Edgeworthstown are taken from the Ballitore Papers in the National Library. The surviving Poor Law Records for South Tipperary form the background for the chapter on Workhouse women. Although I have drawn each of the remaining 'lives' from published material, in each case the books from which they are drawn have long been out of print and their subjects in danger of being forgotten. That would be a tremendous loss to all those interested in Irish history, and in the lives of Irish women in particular.

Nellie Ó Cléirigh

December 2002.

Historical Background

1801 Union of Great Britain and Ireland begins.

1803 Rising of Robert Emmet. His trial and execution.

1808 Journey of Mary Beaufort to the West to inspect the Charter Schools.

1817 Diary of Selina Crampton of life in Merrion Square, Dublin.

1829 Catholic Emancipation Act.

1831 National Schools system instituted.

1836 Irish Constabulary (the Peelers) founded by Robert Peel, British Prime Minister.

1837 Queen Victoria's reign begins.

1838 The Poor Law Act setting up the workhouses.

1845 Start of the Great Famine.

1846 Complete destruction of the potato crop. (Aug-Sept).

Central Relief Committee of Society of Friends (The Quakers) set up in November.

1847 February. Soup-kitchens system established. Famine at its height.

1848 Young Ireland Rising in Munster.

1849-50 Emigration as described by Margaret McCarthy in "The Emigrant's letter".

1867 Fenian Rising

1870 Gladstone's first Land Act. Home-rule movement launched by Isaac Butt.

1879 Irish National Land League founded in Dublin 21st October.

1879-82 The Land War.

1881 The Land Commission established.

Hardship and High Living

1886 Lord Aberdeen becomes Viceroy for six months.

1891 Congested Districts Board set up the British Government to improve conditions in the poorer counties.

1906 Lord Aberdeen returns to Ireland as Viceroy.

1908 Formation of Sinn Fein.

1914-18 The Great War

1915 End of Aberdeen's viceroyalty.

1916 Easter Rising in Dublin.

1919 Dail Eireann adopts provisional Constitution and Declaration of Independence and elects De Valera president of Dail Eireann.

1919-20 Anglo-Irish War including Black and Tan and Auxiliaries involvement.

1920 Government of Ireland Act, providing for separate parliaments and governments in Northern Ireland and Southern Ireland.

1921 Anglo-Irish Treaty

1922 Treaty approved by Dail Eireann. Irish Free State constitution adopted. Civil War begins.

1923 End of Civil War. Period of Cecilia Saunders-Gallagher's imprisonment in Kilmainham Jail.

Chapter One
The Tourist

Mary Beaufort's tour of Connemara in 1808.

No matter how tedious or troublesome your journey to any part of Ireland today, you will travel in total luxury compared with Mary Beaufort's journey in 1808 from Collon in County Louth to Killala and on through Mayo and Galway to Portumna. Mary travelled in the family coach with her husband, Daniel Augustus, her daughter, Louisa, and a servant, who was probably the coachman.

Mary's husband, Daniel Augustus, was Church of Ireland Rector of Collon in County Louth when this journey was undertaken for him to inspect the Charter Schools. Charter Schools were established by the Incorporated Society in Dublin for Promoting English Protestant schools in Ireland; they received a Parliamentary grant and their aim was overtly proselytising. The Charter Schools aimed to give "plain and proper notices of religion" and "qualify the children for the lower orders of life".

Mary was an observant diarist. She was 69 when she made the journey to Connemara. She must have been a strong determined person because she took part in most of the excursions made by the party, this despite the fact that she suffered from varicose ulcers and scabies and had suffered a slight stroke in 1804[1]. The trip to the West covered 579 miles in August and September and must have been an endurance test.

Daniel Beaufort was more than just a clergyman. He was interested in improving farming methods, gardening, and was an amateur cartographer. He laid out demesnes, planned houses, traced genealogies, identified plants and trees and he even sent up hot air balloons. Daniel was a friend of Richard Griffith who master-minded the Ordnance Survey; was a member of the Dublin Society and the Royal Irish Academy; he was described by Maria Edgeworth, the novelist to whom he was doubly related, as "an excellent clergyman of a liberal spirit and conciliating manners"; he was also "a man of taste and literature" and " a lover of good food and wine and a man of decided views on architecture and the arts". Unfortunately, he was a poor manager of money and left his family in debt.

The Beauforts were a very talented family, the best known being Daniel and Mary's son, Francis, who was the inventor of the Beaufort wind-scale. Louisa, who accompanied her parents on their trip to the West, was an accomplished artist. Because of their background, it is not surprising to find that Mary Beaufort noted in her diary the state of the country, the crops grown and the gardens she visited. Obviously an educated woman, she was interested in antiquities and commented on the ruins she saw, as well as giving a detailed account of some of the houses. She must have been particularly interested in flowers, trees and forests because she comments on their presence or absence. Her diary is very valuable for its description of landlord houses and lifestyles in pre-Famine Ireland. It also shows how many Anglo-Irish families were related. The poverty of the ordinary people, the over-population and the fact that only Irish was spoken throughout the West, all help to give us a vivid picture of life at the beginning of the nineteenth century.

Daniel and Mary Beaufort
(from *The Hopeful Traveller, Boethius Press 1987*)

Chapter One: The Tourist

The amount of information about the Charter Schools included in the diary is relatively small but does show that they concentrated on teaching skills rather than a literary education.

Travellers at this time could expect to receive a welcome from families to whom they were known or had letters of introduction. Some of the families visited by the Beauforts were related to them. A welcome in a private house must have been very important when the Beauforts had stayed in inns, almost all of which seem to have been very poor. As the entire diary is not used, a map has been drawn to show the route of their travels. Mary's home, Allentown, as well as Mitchelstown, Barbavilla, and Wilson's Hospital were all private houses sufficiently important to be marked on a large scale Ordnance Survey map.

Mary Beaufort began her travel journal on 29th August, with the following entry:

> We, that is Mr Beaufort, Louisa and I, set out from Collon after breakfast; weather very showry. Arrived at Allentown in good time; found all as well as we would expect them to be. The 31st we proceeded on our journey; paid a visit to Mr Tighe, Mitchelstown, and found them at home and the Henry Wynnes and Mr and Mrs Hamilton on a visit there. Mrs Tighe's garden was laid out by herself and is very pretty; part of it was formerly a pigsty not many years back. There are in it a variety of shrubs and foreign trees and a view of a richly wooded area and fine country. The house is small and neat and the grounds very pretty and well wooded with large fine trees.
>
> Thursday. We went to Barbavilla; met several friends next morning. Left Barbavilla and directing our course to Edgeworthstown we passed through what was once termed "the crooked wood", a very beautiful wood on the side of a hill; it is now completely cut down, not a tree left but a few straggling whitethorns and hollies. Stopped at Wilson's Hospital for a short time. Arrived at Edgeworthstown in time for dinner. We remained there a whole week which time we did not regret on account of the badness of the weather.[2]

Hardship and High Living

Thursday 8th. We left our friends there and proceeded to Longford, stopping at the Charter School on the way. It appears but a poor building. While there we saw what our servant called a rainbow, but it had only the colours of one; it was not in the form of a bow but a large mass, which moved slowly on, over a hill called Corry Clan La and was occasioned by a shower falling between us and the spot where the sun was shining on the hill.

To Longford the road is not either pleasant or good; near the town are more trees; it is an old and ugly town with a poor dirty Inn. There is still remaining the house where the Pakenham family formerly lived. The grandfather of the present Earl built their current residence which the present Lord Longford has altered to a castle, very much to the advantage of the house, both in comfort and appearance.

Passed through Castle Forbes, a poor village, which has no appearance of industry and does not show that its great landlord lives about a quarter of a mile from it. A delay because the iron which supported our lap-box broke. A crowd of children gathered round us and in about a dozen, we did not see one that was not ugly; squalid, naked, half-starved wretches.

Lord Granard's appears a fine place, with many old trees. The road was very bad for some part. We soon discovered the Shannon at a distance. Would be much handsomer if it were not intersected with a number of eel weirs.

Proceeded to Aghamore, the only halting place between Longford and Carrick and it is so small and so poor and so little like a house to put up for the night at, that we had very nearly passed it bye. Shown in to a small dirty dark room just close to the passage and front door, with a bed in it. The room was accepted and the landlady assured the travellers that it was "well aired". We were much better off than we had expected as we got a very good supper and comfortable beds, but for the noise of other folks in the house we should have been better off then in a more sumptuous place. At near ten, Mr.

Chapter One: The Tourist

Caldwell and Col. Prat sent to know if we would allow them to sleep in our parlour in which there was a turn-up bed, beside that in which Mr B. was to sleep----these gentlemen were sitting in the kitchen drying themselves, having come in a gig from the fair of Moyle and this was our unpleasant request. However, it was complied with, provided they waited till the ladies were gone to their apartments.

The travellers crossed the Shannon at Drumsna and travelled on past Jamestown, a formerly walled town. They arrived at Carrick-on-Shannon and were less than impressed by what they found:

Arrived at Carrick-on-Shannon belonging to Mr. St. George. A miserable-looking town, so poor and houses looking so dirty, particularly the inn, that we preferred going on seven miles to breakfast.

They then arrived in Sligo, which appeared equally underwhelming:

To Sligo where we stayed at Nelson's Hotel, at the foot of the Bridge. It is not a neat or well-appointed Inn but the beds and apartments are pretty good and the people obliging.

Sligo streets are narrow, no foot paths and little paving; streets ill let and very few gentlemen's houses and not one handsome shop. The whole town has a shabby appearance, not one handsome public building; the church is large and stands high but is very plain. An immense sized chapel has lately been erected and must have been very expensive for its size but has nothing ornamental in or about it. The Roman Catholic religion prevails amongst the lower orders; Presbyterians and Methodists also abound; the population is great, 12,000 at least. The Session House is under repair and several houses are building, none very good or large. There are several small ships in the river; large cannot come up to the quays. The navigation is bad and rocks are pointed out by long poles, which are thick near them; the quays are short; on one is a Linen Hall which seems well attended; it was so crowded, being Market Day, that we did not attempt to do more than walk up to it; on the quay opposite is a very nice clean-looking, well built shambles. Rain forced us to take shelter in a booksellers and we were very much surprised to find a good collection of very elegantly bound books, many of them in binding we had not before seen; there was none in half binding. Mr Grey, the bookseller, said nobody would buy them if not handsomely bound. He imports them all at little more expense than he would have them printed and bound in Ireland.

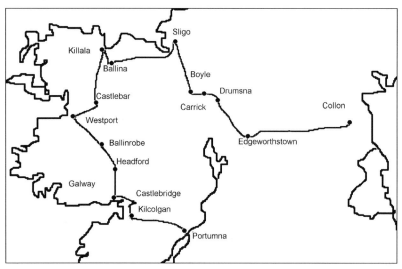

Map of Mary Beaufort's journey through Connaught

When in Sligo, the party visited Hazelwood, the estate of the local landowner, Richard Wynne.

Mr Wynne's grounds are very pretty, a large park all dressed, abundance of trees, a fine lake, and sublime mountains. The house is very heavy consisting of a square centre part and wings. The hall is a pretty room, used as such in summer and furnished accordingly with sofas and family pictures. Lady Sarah and all her company and family were there waiting for us and we all walked out taking the garden on our way. It is a very good one and kept in remarkable order, neat and free from weeds. There was a fine datura in the hot house, not against a wall, and looking very healthy with several very promising flower buds. There was also a large

Chapter One: The Tourist

Volkmeria full of blossoms. A myrtle covered one corner outside and many arbutus.

We saw a variety of walks, a grotto, a reading room and a moss-house. Lady Sarah picked nectarines and flowers for us. She and the children returned to the house and we sailed on the lake, five miles across in one place. All very beautiful including Church Island which promised a good crop of hay and is part under corn. All very wooded. One island had a cottage intended for her ladyship but it was destroyed by rats who ate the thatch. Ancient oaks. We sat down to dinner about seven. There was not much conversation and the ladies retired to the drawing-room pretty early and the gentlemen soon followed after; then tea and we were summoned to prayers read by Richard Wynne; it was now near eleven and no appearance of supper so we ordered our carriage and were not asked to stay nor to meet Mr Edgeworth who was expected there next day.

They were however very obliging and civil. Mr. Wynne is of a reserved and distant disposition, Lady Sarah very easy and affable.

The travellers left Sligo and headed on to Killala via Ballina. The latter part of the journey was especially arduous.

We were told it was but six miles to Killala, of good road and not hilly so we proceeded on. The first mile is good and fine hedge rows on each side of it, but as night came on everything looked gloomy, the country looked ugly, and the road became bad and we became uneasy -- never did six miles appear so long or so bad, hills excessively steep, rugged and broken. We feard everything and felt as if we were to be swallowed in a gulph at every step.

At length after two hours and a half driving we came to the suburbs of Killala and were told the Bishop's Castle was at the near end and presently the great gate appeared; we drove into a court yard, saw numerous lights in the house and many servants appeared, ushered us into a spacious hall, where Mrs Stock[3] soon came, introduced herself and in an obliging manner welcomed us and led us up a handsome pair of stairs, where we met the bishop and most of the family, who all seemed delighted to see us and said they had been very anxious for our coming, that they might be acquainted with us. Mrs Stock busied herself in the most eager manner calling for tea in another room and then after our comfortable tea and good plumb cake we returned to the large drawing-room and played a "Pool of commerce", a game the bishop likes; he says it takes in so many young people. A small supper was spread in the small drawing-room and at a little past eleven we all went to bed.

Whilst there, the Beauforts visited many famous ruins in the area, including those of Moyne Abbey and Rosark Abbey. As guests of the bishop, they also met the gentry of the locality.

We returned home and had but time to hustle on our cloathes for dinner, to which came in addition to our family, Mr and Mrs Edwin Stock, the bishop's eldest son and his wife, a very pleasing couple. His daughter, Maria, married her first cousin Mr Palmer, a clergyman; they also came in the evening and a Mr and Mrs Nesbit and a Captain Lecky. We were a large company for the bishop's family consist of three unmarried daughters, and two sons. He has four more sons, in different employments and professions, all but one is likely to do very well; that one, from some accidental cause, is in a melancholy state of mind. The doctors say he will, in time, with care retrieve his senses . The three girls are well informed, pleasing, sensibly cheerful. One of them is a very pretty girl. They were all very affable and agreeable. Mrs Stock is very obliging. She is much engaged in her household matters and her special study seems to be to please the Bishop and make him happy and he appears very much so.

Other excursions included a trip to a Druid's altar (which is scientifically described by Mary Beaufort) and Bartra Island, owned by the landlord Knox.

Chapter One: The Tourist

Saturday 17th. A party was proposed to sail in Captain Lecky's boat to the Island of BARTRA, better than a mile distant and to fetch cold meat and dine. The island belongs to Mr. Knox (Knox vomica); is pretty and at least in some parts planted; it is said to be above 300 acres, but of arable or grass land for use, there is not above a hundred acres; there is a prodigious quantity of land thrown up, whole ridges of it which is fast increasing and in which rabbits live and become in the season very profitable .

There is a good thatched house here with good pleasant drawingroom and parlour, several bedrooms and all furnished. Mr Knox passes a small portion of his time here on account of his having a public appointment. There are two walled gardens and good offices. Plenty of fish are caught here. Just before we landed, a large take of what they called Greek herring or horse mackerel was brought on shore. They resemble mackerel more than herring, both in size, colour and taste. The poor people salt and keep what is not for present use and find these fish and cockles, which come in much abundance, a great relief to them. We had some of them at our dinner and found them very good.

We were a large party and dined in Mr. Knox's parlour and had our potatoes and our fish. We dressed in his kitchen. We were all of us pleased and wishing to please. As soon as the tide had retired sufficiently to allow us to cross the sands we mounted our gigs, our jaunting car and our tandem, having first seen the sun set in the most glorious and beautiful manner. This, though called an island, is only so when the tide is in. It has about thirty families inhabiting it and hay, corn, meadow and potatoes are grown. A neck of land containing about three acres I hear, Mr. Knox gives free of rent to the present possessor, who is to supply his table with fish.

The Beauforts left for Castlebar, and took in various sights, including Deele Castle, the home of the rakish Lord Tyrawley, who fathered several children by his mistress before eventually marrying her. Castlebar seemed as unkempt as other towns in Mayo.

Westport House
(Courtesy of Westport House & County Park)

Arrived at Castlebar. The town looks shabby and is gone much into decay. It belongs I believe to Lord Lucan who lives entirely in England and does not trouble his head about it other than to receive his rents. His own house is become a barracks, his fine grounds and walks behind it are neglected, his garden let and whatever can increase his rents is turned to profit.

We admired the fine buildings around the square. A little further on stands the Charter School. It is kept by an English woman who was formerly governess to Mrs Cullen and to Mrs Cleaver; was much esteemed by the Wynne family and she and her husband are respectable people and are very attentive to the children. She teaches them to work fine works as well as coarse. The inn is not either good or clean but the people are so civil and so ready to accommodate you that one cannot find fault.

When very near the town of Westport, from a hill just above it, is a view of the town rising on the side of a high hill; the river at the bottom with its two very handsome and well-built quays and a very handsome house of Col. Brown's on an eminence to the right. As you descend into the town you lose but little of its beauty; the richness continues. You see more of Lord Sligo's trees and lawns with the house at a greater distance. The hotel was built and furnished by the Marquis (of Sligo) and for some years the profits went to him; but he was soon tired of this daily trouble and he let it to a clever man who had been steward to a man-of-war. He pays the Marquis so much a year and makes what profit he can out of it. It is a very handsome house, has a coffee house at next door, then a bakery and a range of shops all in symmetry. It has a handsome cut-stone portico and a piazza and all along the quay handsome-looking houses. There are two bridges, one each side of the inn, and on the opposite side, between these two bridges, is a large handsome chapel, a house for the Titular Bishop and another for the parish priest. But the bishop died before his house was finished and his dead body took possession of what was to have been his living residence. No bishop has since been appointed and the house is let to a family.

The Beauforts stayed in the local inn, which they found "clean and comfortable" but rowdy due to the large number of sea-bathers staying there. These were visiting the hot and cold baths erected by Lord Sligo. Lord Sligo's own home and estate was very imposing.

Lord Sligo's house is very large and rather heavy; it stands on an eminence at the head of the port, which, by its position, shows little more than the masts of the shipping, none of the disagreeable parts. The house has been built at different times and round a square court, which the present lord has roofed and by it has made a very handsome addition to his house. He has added at the back a range of buildings the whole breath of it and this continues to apartments for the upper servants. It may be called a mass of building, rather heavy. It is of grey hammered stone.

Clew Bay from Westport
(Engraving from drawing by W.H. Bartlett. Author's Collection)

In the farmyard every thing is on a prodigious large scale. The farm-yard cost £10,000 and contains a house for his steward large enough for a Glebe House for a living of £500 a year; also there are lodgings or dwelling places for forty labourers and workmen and gardeners. There is ground to supply them with vegetables, for he feeds them all. Seven acres apportioned for this purpose. Within this enclosure also are sixteen Bublock houses and various other offices and shops as he calls them, for he makes all his own mechanicks and is ready to sell to the country people any tool or garden seed, or milk or butter. His dairy is large and lined with white tiles, with a marble fountain in the centre. Lady Sligo used to take pleasure in showing her dairy and had two sets of utensils for it, one of china for Great Folks inspection, another of Wedgewoods for lesser gentry and now that her ladyship is become nervous and that she takes pleasure no longer in it, the common ware are in use. There was a vast quantity of milk in it when we, by chance, seeing the door open, looked in.

After looking at stables, coach house, and everything we went to the garden, which contains eight acres walled in, in different compartments, but the appearance is dull. The forest trees seem neglected and not one peach or pear tree on them. The grape houses were full and as fine bunches as could be seen; very few pines, no exotics, not any pretty flowers, or anything but common geraniums.

The Beauforts travelled on to Ballinrobe, which suffered the neglect of its landowner, Lord Tyrawley. Looking at the desolate landscape, Mary frequently wondered how people managed to survive there at all.

One must wonder why people are induced to live in a place to all appearances so uncomfortable, yet this whole country is thickly inhabited and in many parts their industry is picking up loose stones and either building walls or raising piles of them to clear the ground; here and there are small patches of corn.

The group next travelled further south through Ashford and Cong, visiting all the local antiquities before heading towards Galway. This part of the journey afforded few comforts.

The road to Galway was black, rocky and thickly inhabited, where firing was very scarce. We passed a few gentlemen's houses and a great number of ruined houses, castles and abbeys between the Neale and Headfort.

We stopped at Morris, the only place between Headfort and Galway that we could get oats. A vile odious place, a single house on the roadside, bleak and cold, without shelter and the first sentence a stupid-looking man uttered was to say there was no oats for our horses only new oats on the sheaf. But there was no alternative, our horses must rest and eat so out we stopped and into a miserable room, cold and comfortless, without a fire, or even a chair to sit upon. So we adjourned to the kitchen and sat with the wind blowing strong upon us from the open door.

Mary Beaufort's account is often gossipy and good natured. When describing the approach to Clarinbridge, she takes the opportunity to recount the tale of a local scandal.

> Kilcolgan and Clarinbridge were near. The first is a well-looking house built in the castle style by Mr St. George's father, who lives there, keeps a chère ami and to please her turned Roman Catholic. A story is told of this dissolute old gentleman, which one can scarcely credit, that the first day he went to Chapel, it happened that the host was then elevating, at which everyone kneels; he supposed this obeisance was performed in honour of him, bowed all round, and when service was over he came forward and made a fine harangue, returning the congregation thanks for their great civility to him!

> It must be an unpleasant circumstance to his son, who is a moral domestic county gentleman, to have his father living so near him (not two miles from his gate) so despicable a life. The old gentleman built the house and an excellent one it is, finished it in the best manner, with painted ceilings to all the lower rooms and to the hall which is large and handsome. He furnished it in the best style of those days, of about twenty years back, lived in it and enjoyed it and nine or ten years ago resigned it to his son, who soon after married Lady Harriet St. Lawrence and they have lived very happily and have seldom left it, never for any length of time. They have six fine little girls and they appear very happy.

Chapter One: The Tourist

Portumna Castle
(Drawn by Samuel Lover Esq. The Office of Public Works.)

A visit to the area was not complete without a trip to Lord Clanricarde's castle at Portumna.

> We followed a gravel path from the church a short distance to the castle. We were all of us disappointed at the first view of this very antique castle; it stands on a flat and is an immense pile of building. We passed on through a Gothic door, which led to the front; before it is a broad flagged sort of terrace, to which you mount by several steps; there is a ponderous carved door and huge stone door case. The governess told me we could be admitted so we boldly knocked, and were soon answered by a smart-looking servant, who admitted us immediately, and ordered the housekeeper to attend.
>
> We entered a capacious hall; an ornamental screen had been begun of carved wood to separate the doorway and keep off any wind from the fire place but the Lord fell into a bad state of health and the work stopped. Over a large fire place is a stately chimney piece of black marble and a piece of sculpture above it of three

25

figures nearly as large as life representing faith, hope and charity. These and the decorations reach almost the top of this lofty hall. There were other emblems and family banners placed there. We stepped from the Great Hall into the Eating Parlour, a large lofty room with two fireplaces. The windows are high and narrow, not pointed, very distant from the ground, which gives it a gloomy appearance; the ceiling is rich and heavy, not coloured, the wainscot dark red, and beyond it is a breakfast-room and my lord's dressing-room and other chambers. They are all fitted up in a most appropriate castle style and there are several family pictures.

A wide dark oak staircase leads you to the second story, where there is a suite of bedchambers, well furnished, with back stairs and variety of exits. Over the Great Hall is the Grand Drawing Room, of an uncommon length and well proportioned; the ceiling is extremely high with a very deep frieze to which the chimneypiece, a huge one of black painted stone, reached. The breath is in proportion, the windows are square, not large, the frames of stone and the panels of the lower half of the window shutters are looking glass, which had a beautiful effect.

Mary Beaufort concluded her journey with a trip to stay with friends in Castlegar, at which point she ends her account of a somewhat arduous trip through Connacht.

Chapter Two
The Surgeon's Wife

Selina Crampton.

The diary[4] for the year 1817 written by Selina Crampton of Merrion Square, Dublin, is in complete contrast to the diary of Mary Beaufort of her visit to Connemara. It is quite obvious that Selina is not nearly as intelligent as Mary Beaufort, nor is she as well educated. She seems to have been a careful and competent housekeeper. The food served in the house shows a much wider menu than one would have expected. Turkey was eaten quite often, though not on Christmas Day. The range of imported fruits served to guests and the variety of fish eaten is also surprising.

Where the Beauforts were interested in antiquities, buildings, scenery, agriculture and gardening, Selina Crampton's diary gives a graphic account of the life-style of the wife of a successful Dublin surgeon. Her entire life was dedicated to the running of a large household, her social life, her health and that of her family.

Selina's husband, Philip Crampton (1777-1858) was the son of Dr. John Crampton, King's Professor of Materia Medica and Pharmacy, of 12 Gardiner Place, Dublin, so he came from a medical background. The Cramptons were descended from a Nottinghamshire family settled in Ireland in the reign of Charles II. Philip studied medicine in Dublin, entered the army medical service, and left it in 1798 when he was elected surgeon to the Meath Hospital. In 1800 he graduated in medicine in Glasgow. He soon after commenced to teach anatomy in private lectures and maintained a dissecting room behind his own house. For many years he was Surgeon-General to the forces in Ireland and Surgeon-in-ordinary to the Queen, a member of the Senate of the Queen's University and three times President of the Dublin College of Surgeons. A founder of the Royal Zoological Society of Ireland, he secured a grant to it of the ground in Phoenix Park.[5] He was created a baronet in 1839.

Hardship and High Living

Older Dubliners will remember the Crampton Memorial at the junction of Pearse Street, College Street, and D'Olier Street. It was erected to the memory of Philip Crampton because he was the instigator of the provision of a fresh water supply for Dublin city.[6]

Philip Crampton
(Archive Department Adelaide and Meath Hospital)

When Selina wrote her diary, in 1817, she was the wife of a very successful surgeon, mother of seven children, and mistress of a large house in Merrion Square as well as their country house in Merrion Avenue. She was born Selina Cannon and was married in 1800 at St. Peter's Church of Ireland, Dublin.[7] According to Cameron's History of the College of Surgeons, Selina was the third of eight daughters of Patrick Hamilton Cannon, an officer of the Twelfth Dragoons. It appears that Selina was very pretty and that her face was her fortune.[8]

Chapter Two: The Surgeon's Wife

The children mentioned in Selena's diary range from Philly, the eldest girl, who was probably about sixteen, to Johnny and Jos, Minny, Selina, Charlotte and "little Adelaide".

The directories for the period list the Cramptons as residing at 13, 14 and even 15 Merrion Square.[9] This discrepancy is easily accounted for because the houses in Merrion Square were re-numbered several times. According to the History of the Royal College of Surgeons in Ireland, Philip Crampton resided for about 45 years in No. 14 Merrion Square. This house is four stories over basement and has two windows at the side of the hall door. It was famous for the pear tree growing along the front of the house.[10]

Being mistress of a large establishment, Selina had a busy life but she had a large staff both in Merrion Square and at their "country residence" in Merrion Avenue, Booterstown, Co. Dublin, to see to the smooth running of both houses. The children moved "to the country" at Merrion Avenue for the summer months. Selina travelled between the two houses and kept a watchful eye on both. She went to the markets to order the food for her large establishment and paid all the bills at the shops.

Selina entertained both family and medical and social contacts; visitors to breakfast are recorded regularly, large and smaller dinner parties, supper parties sometimes for those who had already dined and extra guests, parties after the theatre, and one very large gathering of 200 persons. Some of the guests were family and extended family, but others are identifiable as prominent in medicine and government. "Belissa", mentioned regularly in the text, is Philip Crampton's sister who married John Smyly K.C.[11] and whose daughter-in-law, Ellen Franks, was the founder of Mrs Smyly's Homes and Schools.

Other visitors to the Crampton household included Drs. James Macartney (1770-1843) and John Cheyne (1777-1836), both of whom had a world-wide reputation. John Creighton was surgeon to the Foundling Hospital and several others. Joseph Stringer was Staff Surgeon at the Royal College of Surgeons.[12] The La Touches were members of the banking family; both Richard and James Ponsonby were members of the Dublin Society and George Ponsonby was a member of the Privy Council. Charles Kendall Bushe of 5 Ely Place and Kilmurray, Thomastown, was Solicitor

General.[13] The best known of all those entertained by Selina was Robert Peel, then Chief Secretary. He became Prime Minister of England in 1834 and again in 1841 but in Ireland he is remembered as the man who set up the Police Force, the Royal Irish Constabulary, commonly known as "the Peelers".

No. 14 Merrion Square in modern times
(Courtesy Brian Siggins, Author's Collection)

Being Surgeon General, Philip's duties included attending on the Lord Lieutenant, the King's Representative in Ireland. This involved almost daily visits to the Viceregal Lodge, today Áras an Uachtaráin, in Phoenix Park, where he often dined. The family were invited to many official Castle functions which Selina records attending. The

Chapter Two: The Surgeon's Wife

Cramptons seem to have been personal friends of Charles Whitworth, the Lord Lieutenant, and his wife and were sincerely sorry when the Whitworths left Ireland in 1817.[14]

Apart from the entertainments she gave, Selina often went to dine in other houses and was quick to comment on the quality of the company and the food. The family were regular theatre goers and again Selina left an account of what amused her and what did not.

Selina's diary gave some idea of Philip Crampton's practice. Most days "he went about his business" in his carriage or tilbury visiting individual patients or attending hospitals and the barracks in Portobello in his capacity as Surgeon General. Apart from surgery, he attended patients suffering from fevers. He also saw "considerable numbers of patients" in the house in Merrion Square, including male patients on a Sunday morning. It is quite possible that he operated at home. The picture of an operation in a Dublin drawing-room in 1817, the year of Selina's diary, is believed to include a drawing of Philip Crampton who was related to Richard Power of Kilfane House, the patient in the picture.[15]

Selected excerpts from Selina's diary have been chosen to show her daily life.

Because Selina usually entered the time she got up, had meals and went to bed this information is not included in all the accounts. Her diary has a page allotted to each day but is not consistent in giving the date or month. The date is given where it is included in the diary or where it is obvious from other pages of the text. Where the places visited by Selina are identifiable the information about them is shown in brackets. Selina's spelling has been retained. The diary gave the dinner menu for every day of the year, but only selected menus are included here.

Selina began her diary for 1817

> 1st January. This day I staid at home the greater part of the morning and then went out for a short time. Philip and Philly (her eldest daughter) and I dined at John's (probably John Crampton Esq. 15 Merrion St.) to meet the bridal party (presumably Philip Cecil Crampton who married Sidney Mary Browne in 1817). Guests included Mr and Mrs Estrinch, General and Miss Fyers, Miss Lee, Miss Rogers, and Belissa. We all went home very

early. We had rather a stupid day. Philip talked of his hunt the day before with Mr. Garnet. He is much better in his stomach since hunting. We had for dinner soup, salmon, roast beef, boiled turkey, ham and a veal pie. Then a plumb pudding, and a custard pudding. Wild duck and maccarroni, mince pies and apple pie. At home dinner for the children and servants was boiled beef and fricasse chicken and rice pudding. We all went to bed at 11 o'clock. The servants had punch in the kitchen and sat up rather later. All the family, thank God, well.

Interior of 14 Merrion Square in modern times
(Courtesy of Seamus Daly)

2nd January, Thursday. This day I staid at home the greater part of the morning in making preparations and giving out every thing necessary for a large dinner party tomorrow. I then went out in the carriage to order several things and dined afterwards at home. Charlotte and Mrs Austin and Mr. Richard Ponsonby dined with us; they did not go away till 10 o'clock. Rather a pleasant day. Philip is very well and all the children. I get up every morning at 8 o'clock and have breakfast at half past 8; Philip about 10 o'clock. We had for dinner a pair of boiled fowl, a ham, roast beef, and pigeon pie and vegetables, woodcocks, apple pie and custards, and maccarroni. Very inconvenient getting dinner dressed, the cooks being at work in the kitchen. I think Philip rode all this day about his business. He had this night no sickness or palpitations in his heart, thank God, although we sat chatting over the fire till near 12. The children went (to bed) at ten.

3rd January, Friday. Up before 9 and at breakfast; extremely busy with Claval all day dressing the dinner and in giving everything out and preparing the rooms and also for the supper. Philip rode all day about his business. I did not go out. We had a party of 18 to dinner consisting of the following persons: Dr. and Mrs Cheyne, Dr. and Mrs Crampton, Dr. and Mrs McCartney, Mr. and Mrs Todd, Mr. Carroll, Mr. Stringer, Dr. Edward Percival, Philip Crampton, Mr. Deane, Mr. Adams, Sir Charles Giesceke (Professor and Lecturer in Minerology). In the evening Mr. and Mrs Estwich, Ann Fyers, the Misses Lee, the Misses Rogers, Mr. and Miss Doyel (sic), Capt Shanley, Mrs and Miss Richards, Miss Whitty, John and Willian Smyly, Mrs Major Crampton, Anne and her two brothers, Letty Doherty, Mrs Doherty, and John Carroll. Mrs Dalton and John Connolly. They danced a little. Neither Miss Byrne nor Miss Griffith sang. They did not go away till one o'clock. Dinner. 2 soups, haddock and salmon patties, mutton pies, sweat breads, mutton cutlets, ham and fowl; roast mutton, roast turkey, barnacle, pheasant, seacale, plumb pudding, jelly, apple tart, raspberry maccarroni.

Supper. Woodcocks, seacale, cold chicken, sliced ham, tartlets, jelly, oranges, apples, raisins, and almonds.

Hardship and High Living

The Crampton Memorial
(Dublin City Public Libraries: Dublin and Irish Collections)

Philip Crampton's work kept him out of the house a good deal and ,when Selina was not looking after domestic arrangements, she took the opportunity to take walks and go out to evening entertainments.

> 7th January, Tuesday. Philip went to hunt at Mr. Garnets and we had breakfast at 1/2 past 8 o'clock for Henry Dawson, John Crampton, and Mr. Stringer. They all went off in John's open carriage at 9 o'clock. I walked at 11 with Johnny and Jos to Finiagles.[16]

> Left Johnny there and walked back with Jos to Miss Maxwells and several other places, then home. I met William Smyly who walked some time with me. At half past 4 o'clock dined, Mr Stringer with us. He went out

with Philip immediately after dinner. Dinner menu: boiled rump of beef, roast fowl and vegetables, snipe, apple pudding, cold beef and 2 fowl.

> Drank tea and went to the play with Belissa and William Smyly. Sat in the side boxes and saw Mr. Braham in "Castle of Andelusia". I did not stay for the farce and was not much entertained. Philip's stomach was much better after hunting and "sweating a great deal". He was out all evening about his business.

And then, again, on the 11th January:

> Saturday. Jos and I walked in the Square; then I went to Miss Pontils, Philly to Miss Lewes and Philip rode to the Infirmary. I took pills and felt very weak and mawkish. Went to the theatre, the opera. Very badly acted and altogether a stupid entertainment. Supper ready for all the party who did not eat any. Dinner was 3 boiled chickens, 2 celery, beef, veg., cold round of beef. Woodcock and pancakes.

Ailments were frequent and illnesses speedily caught, even in a surgeon's family.

> 17th January. John Connolly came to breakfast. Saw the School for Scandal, and the new pantomime acted for the first time by Tom Thumb. Not entertained. Very stupid but the play was good. Philip caught cold and got lumbago, believed to be from wearing a short waistcoat. Dinner: Goose, beef hash, fricasse chicken, salt herrings, stewed apples, and custard.

> 20th January. Took calomel pills and salts to ease myself in a particular region.

> 26th January, Sunday. Brought Mr. and Mrs Dalton to St. Patrick's Church. Our dinner party included John Beresford, Arthur Hume, and Mr. Blaquire. We had a very merry evening jumping and dancing about. Dinner; salmon, mutton broth, sirloin beef, ham, boiled turkey, pigeon pie, veg., wild duck, woodcock, sea kale, maccaroni, plumb pudding, custard, orange jelly, apple pie. Philip had palpitations that night owing I think to a

heavy dinner, to dancing about too much, and to drinking wine and water, before he went to bed.

Given her husband's role as Surgeon General, Selena frequented the highest echelons of Dublin society.

9th February, Sunday. Went to the Castle Chapel (Dublin Castle) and saw the Lord Lieutenant there and the Duchess for the first time this season.

13th February, Thursday. At 8 dressed and went to the Drawing Room (at Dublin Castle) with Philip and Johnny who acted as pages for the first time to the Duchess of Dorsett (this was an important social perquisite). My dress of buff and gold. Very well done.

Throughout February and early March, Selena entertained people such as Lovell Edgeworth, a relation of Maria Edgeworth, and attended events at Dublin Castle and elsewhere. A highlight of the social calendar was St. Patrick's Day.

17th March, Monday. Very busy all day getting my dress ready for Patricks night; then arranged my house cloaths. Dressed for the ball at St. Patricks, a very nice dress of white tabinet trimmed with shamrocks and went with Johnny as a Lyean in his uniform to the Ball. Philip dined at the Castle with Lord Whitworth. We staid to supper and we were very late in getting our carriage so that we did not get to bed till a very late hour.

Then, in April, it was Selena's turn to entertain lavishly.

7th April, Monday. Downstairs very early. Philip was very sick in the night but did not vomit. However I was in a great fright.

I never stirred out all this day and was kept busy all day settling the rooms for a very handsome party which I gave in the evening to the Duchess of Dorsett and a very large company of nearly 200 persons. We had musick first by Mr. and Mrs Dalton and then Retour de Bath by Philly and Miss Doyel and Philip's flute. Then the Echo Song by Miss Greighitti and Philip's flute. There was no more musick. Then three quadrilles were danced and one country dance before supper and a pas de deux, much admired, by little Belissa Smyly; then a waltz by Minny and Belissa. A very handsome supper dressed by Claval. Dancing after supper and they all went away by 4 o'clock. I was much tired.

It would appear from several diary entries that Selena was a nervous and excitable woman, prone to sudden, perhaps psychosomatic illnesses, although we are never given details of the precise cause for her upsets.

27th April, Sunday. I being very ill and most agitated was obliged to take a dose of laudamon again which quieted me. Philip did not get to his dinner til 7 o'clock. He had also to go out after his dinner to Mount Street. He is in extremely low spirits and looks very ill.

28th April, Monday. I awoke rather better this morning and have got myself into rather a more composed train of mind but still very much agitated. I never stirred out this day having watched with the greatest anxiety all day at home for letters but none arrived. The shock I have received has deeply affected my health, my spirits, and appetite being much affected.

Life for the Cramptons was frequently a strange blend of the mundane and the dramatic, as Serena's diary entry for the 19th May demonstrates.

Monday. A gentleman came for Philip to go to Dunboyne to see a Mr. Holmes who was wounded in a duel there. The gentleman is so badly wounded he cannot recover. One of the boys who had a nosebleed the previous night was given senna. After a stupid theatre with the children I went to Mrs La Touche's party at 11.

Again, her entries for 13th and 14th June record side by side the trivial and the profound.

13th June, Friday. Philip went to Edgeworthstown to see Mr. Edgeworth (father of Maria Edgeworth, the writer) who is dangerously ill.

14th June. Saturday. Went to dine at Carton which took 3 hours to get there as we had a pair of tired horses.

They waited dinner for us to 1/2 past 7. Company: Lady Elizabeth Baker, Lady Isabella de Cherbot, Mrs Custer. We spent a very pleasant day and evening and I was delighted with everything I saw. Philip met me there having arrived at 3 o'clock. He had found Mr. Edgeworth dead the night before. A little music.

Sir Robert Peel

Sometimes there were more exotic events to keep the Cramptons occupied.

20th July, Sunday. Philip had his paper to write in the evening. Johnny went with his father to have his teeth cleaned. At a play. Brought 2 of the children to see the Balloon going up at Portobello barracks. Miss Harris also accompanied me and we went in afterwards to a cold collation which the officers of the 11th gave. Saw Mr. Kean in Sir Giles Overcast. Not very great. Did not wait for the farce as usual. Philip spent his evening at Lady Landaffs[17]

Childhood ailments could be particularly hazardous and unpleasant in their treatment, as Selena's entries from early August demonstrate.

> 2nd August, Saturday. Minny complained of a pain in her head and feverishness. I put her to bed immediately and she grew so ill that I was obliged to give her 2 grams of calomel and order senna for her in the morning. Made gooseberry jam.

> 3rd August, Sunday. Uneasy about Minny. We found her very hot and feverish in all respects. She had a rather restless night and raved in her sleep and complained a good deal of one side of her head which, as she had fallen from the top of the press, alarmed me a great deal tho' it had happened 2 days before her illness came on. We put a leech on her temple which bled 4 hours and I think did her a great deal of good."

Minny ultimately made a good recovery.

Perhaps the most important social event of Selena's year was the dinner party she gave for Sir Robert Peel, later Prime Minister of England.

> 12th August, Thursday. I got up at eight this morning and breakfasted immediately. Extremely hurried and tired all day preparing for a dinner party. At 1/2 past 6 they came... Mr. Peel, Mr. Vansittart, Chancellor of the Exchequer of England, his secretary Mr. Sargent, Mr. Strathfield, Col. Pelly, Lord Stachy and Capt. Forbes; Mr. John La Touche, of the banking family, Mr. Abr Hutchinson, Col. and Mrs Brown, Mr. Gregory, Mrs Geo Dawson, Count Torensa, a Venetian nobleman, with Mr. Forbes, and Lord Allen. A very good dinner and a large evening party; excellent musick from Mr. McCartney and Miss Doyell. Philly sang and Philip (played) the flute.

> Supper after and all away at 6. A very elegant party in all respects.

Hardship and High Living

While given to recording in great detail, on some occasions, Selena can be frustratingly enigmatic, as this entry for 23rd August shows. Once again, we are never told the source of her unrest.

> 23rd August, Saturday. I found a letter from Mrs P. (Ponsonby written in pencil) which gave me considerable concern and made me spend an uncomfortable day.

Operation in Dublin drawing room without anaesthetic, 1817.
Philip Crampton is identified as the tall man second from left.
(Archives Department, Adelaide and Meath Hospital)

Whatever the cause, Selena's entries become much sparser from this period onwards, recording little more than the occasional dinner, outings (to see the dancing dogs in the New Tavern at Carlisle Bridge[18]) and visits to friends. A late entry on Christmas Eve shows how severe a mistress Selena could be.

Chapter Two: The Surgeon's Wife

24th December, Wednesday. Went to Milltown Lottery Office. Came home and found no meat had been sent from Captn. Reldens and had to send to market for meat for tomorrow's dinner and for dinner this day. I had a great deal of trouble getting Christmas boxes for the children. The servants are to have none in consequence of the things that have been lost in the house this year.

Not surprisingly, Christmas proved to be a hectic round of social events.

25th December, Thursday. Rather an uncomfortable Christmas Day tho Philip is, thank God, pretty well and all the children except Charlotte who has a slight cold and cough. Philip also in church alarmed me by hemming and spitting a little blood. However, he found it came only from his throat. Hurried myself to make plumb puddings and mince pies for the servants dinner and ours and arranged all and hurried to the Castle Chapel with Philip and the 4 older children. Heard an indifferent sermon from the Dean of Cork, Doc. Magee. Lord Talbott (Lord Lieutenant since September) was at church. I received the sacrament and came home at 10 o'clock and remained there till dinner at 1/4 past 5. Charles Acton and Tom Burke for dinner with me and Mr. McNamara. We spent a very merry evening tho I was a little lost. Philip dined with the Lord Lieutenant at the Lodge in the Park. Mr. Lambert brought him there at 6 and home at 8. Dinner: Roast sirloin of beef, leg, boiled tongue, and greens. Mince pies, 2 plumb puddings and brocoli.

The last pages of Selina Crampton's diary provide some very significant information. They are headed "Money given to me by Philip 1817". The largest monthly amount, £351, was in August and the smallest, £87.13.9. in July. The total for the year was an astonishing £1,750.07. 0.

Despite all his ailments Philip lived to be 81. He is reputed to have boasted that he could swim across Lough Bray, ride into town and amputate an arm before breakfast. Selina appears to have been very devoted to him though one cannot help speculating what she meant in her comment that he "staid out till late as usual".

We can also wonder why Selina was so upset that she took laudanum. Was she a hypochondriac? She seems to have suffered from continual constipation for which she was always taking pills but perhaps a diet of smaller meals might have produced better results. She may have been pregnant.

The Meath Hospital c.1816
(History of the Royal College of Surgeons. Cameron 1926)

Selina's son, John, had a distinguished career in the British diplomatic service. He was Ambassador to Russia at the time of his father's death. His sister, also Selina, was an accomplished amateur water-colourist.

Part of the poignancy of Selena Crampton's journal comes from our knowledge of what happened to her afterwards. The Freeman's Journal of 12th April 1834 tells us of a "Melancholy and Fatal Accident".

> Thursday night, as Mrs Crampton, the lady of the Surgeon General, was reading in her drawing-room, her clothes caught fire; and before her screams brought any of the servants to her assistance, she was so dreadfully burned, that not withstanding the exertions of Mr. Crampton himself, assisted by almost all his professional brethren, and aided by every resource that anxiety could devise or skill suggest, the unfortunate lady languished in great torture throughout the night and expired yesterday morning."

Her husband survived her by another 24 years.

Chapter Three
Good Works

Maria Edgeworth and the Great Famine.

Many contemporary accounts of the Famine stress the horrors, the ineffectual efforts to relieve distress and the resulting emigration, but there are few accounts of efforts by individual landlords to alleviate the situation or of the enormous contribution of the Quaker community to this effort. The letters of the author, Maria Edgeworth, which are included in the Ballytore Papers[19] held by the National Library of Ireland, show the efforts of one family and of the Quaker Relief organisation to deal with the distress in Edgeworthstown, Co. Longford.

Maria Edgeworth was born on 1st January 1768 at Black Bourton, Oxfordshire, in the home of her mother's family. She was the third of five children born to Richard Lovell Edgeworth, whose English family had settled in Ireland. She lost her mother when she was only five years old. Within a short time she acquired a stepmother, Honora Sneyd, who added two more children to her husband's family. When Honora died, in 1780, Richard married her sister Elizabeth, who in time added another nine children to the family.

At the age of eight Maria was sent to school in Derby and later to London, where she remained until her father brought his entire family to live permanently on the estate he had inherited at Edgeworthstown. This was in 1782 when Maria was 14 years old. Her father's estate amounted to 4,500 acres and he also owned most of the houses in the village. He proved a capable and just landlord and magistrate. More importantly, he was a resident landlord when this was very much the exception amongst landowners at the time.

Maria helped her father in the running of the estate; she rode beside him round the area and kept the estate accounts, thus gaining interests and experiences most unusual for a girl of her age and social class.

Maria Edgeworth's best know publication was Castle Rackrent, published in 1800, but she wrote a number of other books and assisted her father in his writing. Her published work made her a lady of independent means, earning her more then £11,000 over the course of her career, a large sum in those days and far more than the £700 earned by Jane Austen in her life-time.

As well as assisting in the management of the estate Maria was involved in the education of her step-brothers and sisters. In all, Richard Edgeworth fathered twenty-two children. His fourth marriage, on Elizabeth's death, was to Frances Beaufort, the daughter of Daniel and Mary Beaufort, whom we have already met in a previous chapter. Frances was a talented artist who had been asked to do the illustrations for a new edition of "The Parent's Assistant", one of Maria's books. When she became Maria's third step-mother she was two years her junior but though Maria opposed the marriage in the beginning, Frances became her close friend and confidant and Maria travelled with her father and step-mother and other family members to England and France on a number of occasions.

On her first visit to Paris Maria met a Swedish gentleman, the Chevalier Edelcrantz, who proposed marriage to her, an offer which apparently surprised her and which she promptly refused. She never married. In her own view her literary pursuits were only part of her life. Her main interest was always her family, its welfare and occupations.

Through incompetence, illness, and the death of some of the male members of the Edgeworth family, the estate ran into financial difficulties and Maria was forced to take over the management. She acted in this capacity from 1826 to 1839 and proved very capable in dealing with some formidable problems. From then onwards the estate was managed by Francis, the son of Richard's fourth wife who lived at Edgeworthstown House with his Spanish wife and their children until his untimely death in 1846. During this period the Edgeworths had trouble with their tenants who, at election times, voted for nationalist candidates against the wishes of the family. Maria understood the deep nationalistic feelings of the people but she belonged to the landlord class and had no sympathy with the view that the land really belonged to the people.

During the first years of the Famine Maria worked hard to relieve local distress. She was 79 years of age when she wrote to the Quaker Central Relief Committee but her mental faculties were as sharp as ever. Her letters to the Committee show she knew what foodstuffs were most suitable for relief distribution in her area and how they should be transported to Edgeworthstown without loss. It is also clear from the correspondence that both soup and clothing were sold at low prices, not distributed free.

Apart from the letters, Maria allowed her name to be widely used in appeals for help. She also wrote a story called "Orlandino" for the relief fund.

Maria Edgeworth
(Dublin Historical Record Autumn 2002)

The Society of Friends, or "Quakers" as they were better known, are remembered as the most important private supplier of relief during the Famine. A Relief Committee was set up in Dublin in January 1846. One of its first actions was to try to find out the scale of the potato blight in each area; a questionnaire was devised for this purpose.

A Quaker Relief Committee was also established in London which solicited subscriptions in England and America. It was agreed to set up soup-shops and to supply boilers freely and to make grants of money in aid. The Quaker relief motto was: "No preference should be made in the distribution of relief on the grounds of religious profession."

Two types of Committee were set up, one to plan and conduct soup kitchens and another to undertake the distribution of clothing. Later, auxiliary Committees were set up in Cork, Limerick, Waterford and Clonmel, all areas where there were strong Quaker communities. Committee members were all volunteers but it became necessary to have a paid secretary and staff of clerks to deal with the large number of applications for assistance.

A further Committee was subsequently set up to purchase flannels, grey calicoes, blue prints, corduroy, guernsey shirts, bed-rugs, cotton shirts and leather for shoes. The materials were made up under supervision and distributed.

Maria Edgeworth's responses to the Relief Committee's questionnaire provide an excellent account of conditions in the Edgeworthstown area. The document was dated 30th January 1847 and was signed by John K. Pomele, Vicar of Edgeworthstown and Secretary of the Relief Committee, Maria Edgeworth and Frances Edgeworth, who was Maria's third step-mother.

According to Maria, the parish of Edgeworthstown extended about six miles and had upwards of 5,000 inhabitants, about 3,000 of whom needed public relief. About 100 able-bodied labourers found employment in the ordinary manner at between 8d and 10d per day. About 400 were employed on the Public Works, the employment schemes set up by the British Government. Maria estimated that their earnings were certainly not sufficient at the current price of food to preserve themselves and their families from want. There were no manufacturers or other indoor productive employment, and no support from fishing. The farms were small and under tillage. The small farmers could not cultivate their land as all their labour went to procure provisions. There was no stock of potatoes, none remaining in the ground, none reserved for seed, and none for sale. It was not expected that any considerable quantity of potatoes would be planted in the coming season.

Family viewing rotten potatoes, August 1846.

Family viewing rotten potatoes, August 1846
(Illustrated London News)

There were very few able-bodied labourers without employment. It was not possible to tell how many persons were incapable of labour if widows, children and old persons were counted, about 500 in the district. Edgeworthstown was in the Poor Law Union of Longford, which was seven miles away and where the Workhouse was full. The last two Poor Rates were 71/2d and 5d, the latter being only partially collected. A Relief Committee had been formed; private subscriptions of £186 and a Government contribution were obtained. The Irish Relief Committee granted £20 for a soup shop. This money had been used in selling food at a reasonable rate to the poor since the previous September.

Two absentee proprietors, C. J. Edgeworth and Mrs Tuite, subscribed £25 and £19 respectively. One resident proprietor and a few large farmers had subscribed to the Relief Fund.

All the families of the poor were visited before relief was afforded; there was a great deal of sickness and some fever. The nearest place where provisions were stored in quantity was Longford, seven miles distant. Prices were 1s for a 4lb loaf, wheaten flour 4s per stone, oatmeal 3s/6d. Indian meal was 3s per stone and beef 5d per lb, mutton 6d.

A soup shop had already been established, where 30 gallons were made trice a week and sold at 1d per quart. Maria Edgeworth pointed out that an increased supply would improve matters if bread could be given without increasing the price.

An "Additional Observation" set out that the want of shoes was great and affected health and the power to labour, especially in draining work. (Much of the Public Works set up by the Government involved drainage).

Maria Edgeworth's letter of 1st February 1847 to Dr. Harvey of the Relief Committee paid tribute to the Vicar, his wife and his sister, Miss Pomele. She continued:

> The main point however is clear, that we are in want.

> After doing and overdoing all we could by subscriptions, exertions in procuring and cooking and administering food to those who have neither health nor employment by which they could otherwise obtain subsistence, or be saved from starving, still we find that it will be impossible for us without aid to continue to support the soup shop, or to buy food in any way, of any kind, sufficient to get through the four ensuing months. We are particularly anxious to enable the poor to work for themselves, when ever health and strength permit, that they may preserve some sense of self respect and some spirit of independence and industry.

> We find among the poorest women and children, even in their present distressed condition, sparks of this good principle of independence. A poor woman the other day in thanking our vicar for the assistance he gave in employing men and boys, according to the government arrangements, regretted that when so much was done for men nothing has been thought of for women or children, who are, as she said, also willing to work; if

they could be employed and paid, they would work to their utmost. If we could be aided by a small sum to buy materials and to pay for women's work, we would set them to such needlework, knitting, etc as would be in some degree profitable in a pecuniary point of view, and in a much greater degree useful both now and hereafter in preventing them from losing the proper sense of shame, or becoming mere beggars and paupers, and sinking into idleness and consequent vice.

Joseph Bewley and Jonathan Pim, Secretaries to the Central Relief Committee of the Society of Friends, Dublin, replied to Maria Edgeworth on 2nd February 1847, with an offer of £30 to encourage "a large increase in the distribution of soup which should be daily. If a larger boiler, say of 70 or 80 gallons, could be kept at work, we would grant one also, and if a Committee be formed for the special object of promoting female employment, the sum of £10 as a grant will be placed at their disposal".

On 5th February Maria Edgeworth responded, thanking the Committee for the grant of £30 but making the point that it would be impossible to distribute the soup on a daily basis.

> We beg leave to observe that the distribution of soup cannot be made daily, as this would interfere with the Catholic Fast Day of Friday, and with the Protestant clergyman's Sunday duty. If made, as it should be, three times a week, your purpose of constant supply will be ensured, by giving double portions on the three appointed days, as the soup can be kept at the poor people's own homes for the intermediate days.
>
> Your offer of a large boiler of 70 or 80 gallons would be superfluous to us, as our Vicar has to keep at work one of a hundred gallons. If instead of a boiler your committee would give us (what I believe would cost them less) a Pepin's Digester, it would be of great service according to Count Rumford's advise; "we could make our bare bones, well digested nourish our fellar creatures".

Referring to the proposed grant of an additional £10 to promote the employment of women in the area, Maria proposed the setting up of a Committee made up of herself, her step-mother, Frances, Mrs

Francis Edgeworth (her sister-in-law), the Local Vicar, Reverend J. Pomele, and his wife and daughter, who would be "answerable for the proper and careful use of the £10 you are so good to grant in aid of their efforts."

A letter from Maria to the Relief Committee dated 15th February deals with the method of payment of the £30 and £10 grants and again requests a Pepin's Digester for making bones into soup. The Committee responded with a promise to lodge £40 in the bank of Hale & Co, to be used for the extension of the soup shop and for 'female employment'. Messrs Bewley and Pim said the "Committee have made the grant in the full confidence that they can depend on thy having the distribution competently arranged and shall be glad to hear that such has been effected. We trust thou wilt be able to purchase a Digester thyself, as we have none of those utensils at our disposal."

The Relief papers of 4th March show that a grant was made to Maria Edgeworth of half a ton of rice at £6. By May 1847 the situation had deteriorated considerably and, on the 5th May, she wrote to the Committee with a request for further aid:

> But for your efficient assistance hundreds of poor in this village, in this neighbourhood, would have actually perished from hunger and now in the perilous changes taking place in consequence of the orders to stop government work[20] and in the delay of payments, and in the difficulty of obtaining employment, many must perish unless we can obtain more means of feeding the absolutely destitute, and to assist those who are able and willing to emigrate, to clear the superabundant population, who cannot be employed … I am informed that fresh supplies of provisions have arrived in Dublin, and are at your disposal - we pray you to grant us a fresh supply of rice and meal and corn and flour. I have received from Mr Everett the head of Cambridge University, Boston, a pamphlet containing his speech and various excellent speeches inviting subscriptions for Irish distress-relief. I will send it to you if you wish. I mention it here however principally to remark that great American subscriptions have I understand been remitted in money, and I trust that also some of these are at your disposal and that you could have the

goodness to assist us with a sum which would enable us to assist those desirous to emigrate. Perhaps you could inform us whether there are any vessels now in Dublin Bay, which take out emigrants from Ireland and at what price per head. The numbers here who are desirous to go out are beyond what I could venture to name to you gentlemen. I must only leave it to good friends to calculate and afford whatever you are able with justice to others.

The Committee were only able to part-grant Maria's request. On 8th May, 1847 they wrote:

The Committee having considered thy letter of application for relief direct us to transmit 4 sacks of Indian meal and an order of Baker, Wardle and Co. for half a ton of rice, to be distributed in a cracked state as far as practicable and when completed to return an account of this ...... distribution and the committee are unable to meet thy wishes as to emigration having no funds at their disposal for that purpose. At present in Dublin Bay are 3 vessels taking passengers to America; the charge we are informed is £7.10.0.

On 22nd December 1847, Messrs Bewley and Pim wrote again to Maria, informing her that they would facilitate the delivery of a consignment of Indian meal, which had been sent by a Relief Committee in Cincinnati and which was on its way to Liverpool, by forwarding immediately an equivalent amount of grain taken from the Government depot in Longford in order to hasten the delivery of much needed food to the starving in the area.

We accordingly forward an order to the officer in charge of the Commissariat of the depot in Longford for 4 1/2 tons of Indian meal, which exceeds by 84 lbs the contents of 57 barrels, supposing them to be full. This excess may be applied likewise to the relief of the poor in thy neighbourhood.

On 20th December Maria wrote to the Central Relief Committee about another similar consignment of meal, pointing out that the food needed to be made secure for fear of theft during transit:

Hardship and High Living

Let me beg that you will have the bung holes of the barrels examined and that you will then make them secure. The former barrels of corn meal and rice sent by canal boat were pillaged, and some stores purloined thro' the bung holes. This is scandalous in Ireland, when the meal is for the relief of the Irish poor, and is a shocking contrast to American consideration for this country and American liberality in great things and small. Of course gentlemen, if any expense attends the securing the barrels from depredation I shall most willingly repay it by P.O. order.

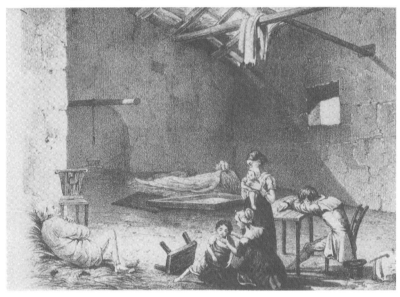

Interior of famine cottage
(Illustrated London News)

As late as 22nd and 29th December 1847 Maria was still corresponding with the Relief Committee about further supplies from the Committee in Cincinnati. This time she received 41/2 tons of meal, which was 84 lbs more than the 57 barrels consigned from America. She wrote on 29th December "I return you my thanks for the gratuitous excess which will, as you kindly suggest, go to the relief of our poor, and it gladdens my heart to receive so much friendship, and witness so much charitable - not only charitable - Christian feeling in every step of these transactions."

The final items in the correspondence deal with the grant of the Relief Committee of 21/2 pieces of flannel, two parcels of leather, one piece of calico and one piece of tweed which were acknowledged on 14th March 1848 by F. Edgeworth in Miss Edgeworth's absence. The latter states that:

> some of the leather was immediately cut out and given to a man, a poor brogue maker, to make up and which he has done for the low price of 1/- per pair and most of them have been sold. The other things were sold at a very, very, low price. I have a small sum on hand the produce of the sales of my part, after paying for the carriage and for the making of the brogues which I send to you by P.O. order.

Maria Edgeworth's old age was healthy and vigorous. Her death came, as she had always hoped and prayed, suddenly and at her home. On the morning of 22nd May 1849 she went for a drive, as was her usual custom. On her return she suffered a heart attack and died within a few hours.

Chapter Four
An Emigrant's Tale

From Ballydesmond to America.

Whereas Maria Edgeworth's account shows us the hardships of the Famine at first-hand, the aftermath of the Famine and the enforced emigration of so many Irish men and women is clearly seen in the letters of Margaret McCarthy, an émigré in America, to her family back in Ireland. The records of assisted emigration from Kingwilliamstown (Ballydesmond today) on the Cork-Kerry border to New York and Buffalo[21] provide a vivid account of the type of journey and the reception that would have awaited Margaret and her party in America.

The British Crown owned an estate at Kingwilliamstown, in the parish of Nohaval Daly, barony of Duhallow, near Kanturk on the Cork-Kerry border. The idea of State-aided emigration for the area originated with Richard Griffith who, when compiling the Ordnance Survey, recommended in April 1849 that a scheme should be devised "for the removal of the surplus population" from the area.

The estate at Kingwilliamstown, along with land in Roscommon, Galway, and Kerry, was administered for the British Crown by its agency, the Commissioners for Woods, Forests, and the Land Revenue of the Crown. The local agent in Kingwilliamstown was Michael Boyan, who was also in charge of a model farm experiment conducted by the State in that area. As a result of Richard Griffith's recommendation, Boyan was instructed to prepare lists of those who would emigrate willingly, or whose compulsory removal was necessary for the "improvements of the estate".

How bad were conditions in the area? The Famine relief provided by the British Government, such as it was, was exhausted by this period. The Treasury, the equivalent of modern Department of Finance, sent a warrant on 6th August 1849 to Boyan authorising the expenditure of £1,000 for removing 238 persons, 158 adults and 80 children, from Kingwilliamstown to New York, at an estimated cost of

£6.15s for each adult and £5.3s for a child. This was approximately the estimated cost of keeping one adult for one year in a Workhouse.

The first party, consisting of 119 people, left Kingwilliamstown for Cork on 30th August 1849. They sailed for Liverpool aboard the "Nimrod" and embarked for New York on 7th September. Kennelly and Company, of 23 Maylor Street, Cork, agents for the Liverpool firm of Harnden and Company, had charge of the travel arrangements. The fare for an adult was £3 and for a child £2.5s. Food or sea-stores were provided and each adult was to receive one pound and each child ten shillings in American currency on landing in New York. A visit to the Emigrant Centre in Cobh will give some idea of what conditions on the journey were like; probably they were worst during the immediate post-Famine period.

The Nimrod
(Illustrated London News)

Even on the journey from Cork to Liverpool some of the emigrants complained that sufficient food was not provided. To add to their difficulties, three persons died at sea between Cork and Liverpool and two sisters were sent home, one because she had not "the use of one leg". In all, only 114 persons sailed from Liverpool in this group.

Some of the emigrants were English-speaking and could write very good English. John Galvin, a mason, wrote to the Commissioners in Ireland complaining that neither he nor his family had received any provisions while in Liverpool or during the voyage to America. Reports from the emigration officer in Liverpool insisted that all the travellers had adequate supplies of food.

The fare for the next group of emigrants was a pound dearer per adult. The list of food to be supplied gives some idea of conditions on these ships but, if fully distributed, the food would have been much better than the diet in Workhouses or in Relief Kitchens. Organised groups such as this one probably fared better than individual travellers.

According to the tender, the food to be supplied to each adult on this voyage was as follows:-

> 3 quarts of water daily
>
> 2 ½ lbs bread or biscuit weekly
>
> 2 lbs rice weekly
>
> 1 lb wheat flour weekly
>
> 3 lbs oatmeal weekly
>
> ½ lbs sugar weekly
>
> ½ lbs molasses weekly
>
> 2 ozs tea weekly

Children under fourteen received half the above quantities.

The Emigration Commission suggested raising the oatmeal allowance to 5 lbs weekly per person and that the shipping agents should be responsible for maintaining the party in Liverpool should any delay occur before sailing.

This second group of thirty-six persons left Cork for Liverpool on 15th June 1850 and arrived in New York shortly before 29th July. A third party of seventeen left Cork on 5th October the same year and the final party of nineteen left on 10th September 1851.

As a result of the assisted emigration, the population of Kingwilliamstown fell from 656 in May 1849 to 479 by November 1852.

The emigrants from Kingwilliamstown seem to have been better off than those from the other areas of this particular State-aided scheme. Darby Buckley, Patrick Connell, Denis Danuhy, Denis Duggan, John Foley and Pat Sullivan were all described as farmers; several of the others were sons or daughters of farmers. A few were labourers; one was the daughter of the caretaker of the model farm.

The people went in family groups, usually a husband, wife and several children.   Sometimes they were accompanied by other relatives like Mary Collins, aged 27, who travelled with her aunt, Mary Guiney, a widow with three sons and one daughter who ranged in age from eight to 23.

Quite a number were known to have stayed in the Buffalo area, including the family of Daniel Daly, aged 50, who died on the voyage from Liverpool to America. Denis Danihy (Matt) of Tooreenclassagh was quite old, 60, when he emigrated. His wife, Johanna, was 50 and their six sons and three daughters, aged 21 to 3 years, all settled in Buffalo.

The most interesting part of the surviving documents are the letters sent home from Buffalo and New York. The accounts of how well the emigrants fared in America may have been exaggerated but showed that conditions for them were certainly better in Buffalo than in Ballydesmond. More than anything else the letters showed how well the Irish looked after their own. Daniel Guiney, writing from Exchange Street, Buffalo, said that his group were met on arrival in Buffalo by Mathew Leary and Dan Danihy, who brought a horse and took their luggage to his house where they had a meal of potatoes, meat, butter, bread and tea. They had drink afterwards in Mathew Leary's house with other families, including that of Conor Leary, who had died in Hospital in Buffalo.

Emigrants Agents' Office
(Illustrated London News)

Chapter Four: An Emigrant's Tale

The arrivals must have had quite a party as they "went to the store and bought 2 dozen bottles of small beer and a gallon of gin otherwise whiskey" and were drinking until morning. Denis Reen had been dressed by Daniel Danihy Matt "with clothes suitable for this country" so that you would think him "a boss or steward". The report does not tell how many of the emigrants could read and write English, but the letters in English, if short on punctuation, showed quite a good standard of literacy and were very entertaining. Daniel Guiney wrote that "as to the girls that used to be trotting on the bogs at home to hear them talk English would be a great astonishment to you ".

A postscript to the letter included the information that Mary Keeffe got two dresses, one from Mary Danihy and the other from Biddy Matt.

The embarkation, Waterloo Dock, Liverpool
(Illustrated London News)

Daniel Guiney described how the group left New York for Buffalo; they sailed out for Buffalo and arrived the following day in Albany. "We left Albany the same day and came out on the canal boat which was drawn by horses. It took us eight days to come to Buffalo which was very expensive for us. Bread and milk were dear along the canal". Guiney sent home a detailed description of the farms they passed "large stocks of cattle, 40 and 50 cows together" then "down to 10 and 12 or 5 and 6". He quoted "You may be sure that we seen great many wonders".

The best of the letters was written on 22 September 1850 by Margaret McCarthy to her family and would have served as an emigrant's guide. She was 22 years of age, the daughter of Alexander (Sandy) McCarthy, carpenter to the Crown estate, native of Boherboy, and Nell, his wife. Margaret sailed from Liverpool on 7th September 1849 on the Columbus and arrived in New York on 22nd October. She settled in New York. A small amount of punctuation has been introduced to Margaret's letter to make it easier to read but her spelling and the use of capital letters has been largely retained.

New York. September 22nd, 1850.

My Dr. Father and Mother Brothers and Sisters

I write these few lines to you hoping That these few lines may find you all in as good State of health as I am in at present thank God. I received your welcome letter To me Dated 22[nd.] of May which was A Credit to me for the Stile and Elligence of its Fluent Language but I must Say Rather Flattering. My Dr. Father I must only say that this is a good place and A good Country for if one place does not Suit A man he can go to Another and can very easy please himself But there is one thing thats Ruining this place Especially the Frontirs towns and Cities where the Flow of Emmigration is most, the Emmigrants has not money Enough to Take them to the Interior of the Country which oblidges them to Remain here in York and the like places for which Reason Causes the less demand for Labour and also the great Reduction in wages.

For this Reason I would advise no one to Come to America that would not have Some Money after landing here that (would) Enable them to go west in case they would get no work to do here but any man or woman without a family are fools that would not venture and Come to this plentyful Country where no man or woman ever Hungered or ever will and where you will not be Seen Naked, but I can assure you there are Dangers

Chapter Four: An Emigrant's Tale

upon Dangers Attending Comeing here but my Friends nothing Venture nothing have.

Fortune will favour the brave, have Courage and prepare yourself for the next time that worthy man Mr. Boyan is Sending out the next lot, and Come you all Together Couragiously and bid adieu to that lovely place the land of our Birth, that place where the young and old joined Together in one Common Union, both night and day Engaged in Innocent Amusement. But alas. I am now Told its Gulf of Miserary oppression Degradetion and Ruin of every Discription which I am Sorry to hear of so Doleful a History to Be told of our Dr. Country. This my Dr. Father Induces me to Remit to you in this Letter 20 Dollars that is four Pounds thinking it might be Some Acquisition to you untill you might Be Clearing away from that place all together and the Sooner the Better for Believe me I could not Express how great would be my joy at our seeing you all here Together where you would never want or be at a loss for a good Breakfast and Dinner. So prepare as soon as possible for this will be my last Remittince untill I see you all here.

Bring with you as much Tools as you can as it will cost you nothing to Bring them And as for you Clothing you need not care much But that I would like that yourself would Bring one good Shoot of Cloth that you would spare until you come here   And as for Mary She need not mind much as I will have for her A Silk Dress A Bonnet and Viel according and Ellen I need not mention what I will have for her I can fit her well. You are to Bring Enough Flannels and do not form it at home as the way they wear Flannel at home and here is quiet different For which reason I would Rather that you would not form any of it untill you Come, with the Exception of whatever Quantity of Drawers you may have you can make them at home But make them Roomly Enough But Make No Jackets.

My Dr. Father I am Still in the Same place but do not Intend to Stop there for the winter. I mean to Come in to New York and there Spend the winter. Thade

Hardship and High Living

Houlehan wrote to me Saying that if I wished to go up the Country that he would send me money but I declined so doing untill you Come and then after you Coming, if you think it may be Better for us to Remain here or go west, it will be for you to judge but untill then I will Remain here.

Dan Keliher Tells me that you Knew more of the House Carpentry than he did himself and he can earn from twelve to fourteen Shillings a day that is seven Shilling British and he also Tells me that Florence will do very well and that Michl can get a place Right off as you will not be In the Second day when you can Bind him to any Trade you wish.

Emigrant ship, between decks
(Illustrated London News)

And as for John he will Be Very Shortly able to Be Bound too So that I have Every Reason to Believe that we will all do well Together So as that I am sure its not for Slavery I want you to Come to here, no its for affording My Brothers and Sisters And I, an oppertunity of Showing our Kindness and Gratitude and Comeing on your Seniour days that we would be placed in that

64

possision that you my Dr. Father and Mother could walk about Lesuirly and Indepenly without Requireing your Labour, an object which I am Sure will not fail even by Myself if I was oblidged to do it without the assistance of Brother or Sister for my Dr. Father and Mother.

I am proud and happy to Be away from where the County Charges man or the poor Rates man or any other rates man would have the Satisfaction of once Impounding my cow or any other article of mine. Oh how happy I feel and am sure to have luck as The Lord had not it destined for (hole in paper probably obliterating "me") to get married to Some Loammun or another at home that after a few months he and I may be an Incumberance upon you or perhaps in the poor house by this. So my Dr. Father according as I had Stated to you I hope that whilst you are at home I hope that you will give my Sister Mary that privelage of Injoying herself Innocently, on any occation that She pleases so far as I have said Innocently and as for my Dr. Ellen I am in Raptures of joy when I think of one day Seeing her and you all at the dock in New York and if I do not have a good Bottle of Brandy for you Awaiting your arrival its a Causion.

Well I have only to tell My Dr. Mother to Bring all her Bed-Close and also to bring the Kittle and an oven and have handles to them and do not forget the Smoothing Irons and Beware when you are on Board to Bring some good flour and Ingage with the Captain Cook and he will do it better for you for very little and also Bring some whiskey and give them to the Cook and Some Sailors that you may think would do you any good to give them a Glass once in a time and it may be no harm.

And Dr. Father when you are Comeing here if you Possibly can Bring My Uncle Con. I would Be glad that you would and I am sure he would be of the greatest acquisision to you on board and also Tell Mary Keeffe that if her Child died that I will Pay her passage very Shortly and when you are Comeing do not be frightened. Take Courage and be Determined and bold in your Undertaking as the first two or three days will be the worst for you and mind whatever happens on board Keep your own temper do not speak angry to any or hasty; the Mildest Man has the best Chance on board so you make your way with every one and further you are to speak to Mr. Boyan and he I am sure will get one Request for you; Mr. Boyan will do it for me. When you are to Come ask Mr. Boyan to give you a few lines to the Agent or berth Master of the Ship that will Secure to you the Second Cabin which I am sure Mr.Boyan will do and as soon as you Receive this letter write to me and let me know about every thing when you are to come and what time and state Particulars of evry thing to me Direct as before. And if you are to come Shortly when you come To Liverpool write to me also and let me know when you are to sail and the name of the Ship you sail in as I will be uneasy untill I get an answer.

No more at present But that you will give Mr. and Mrs Boyan my best love and respect And let me know how they and family are as they would or will not Be ever Better than I would wish them to be; also Mrs Milton and Charles, Mr. and Mrs Roche and family, Mr. and Mrs Day and family, Mr. Walsh and as for his family I sure (hope) are all well, Mr. and Mrs Sullivan and family, Mrs O'Brien, Con Sheehan, wife and family, all the Hearlihys and familys, Tim Leahy and family, Own Sullivan of Cariganes and family, Darby Guinee and family, John Calleghan and family, Timothy Calleghan and family, Timothy Sheehan and Mother.

So no more at present from your Ever Dear and Loveing Child

Margaret McCarthy.

Chapter Five
Between the Walls

The World of Workhouse Women.

Of all the women depicted in these pages, those in Workhouses were the worst off. They were there in sheer desperation and as a last resort; they had no future. Their lives have been vividly described in the research of historian Anne Lanigan[22]

The Poor Relief (Ireland) Act became law on the 31st July 1838. It was the culmination of years of sporadic investigation by the British Parliament into the formidable reality of Irish destitution. Since the Act of Union in 1800 there had been many official inquiries into the nature and causes of Irish poverty but this was the first time that practical measures were adopted with a view to containing this urgent and growing problem.

In introducing the Poor Law to Ireland, the British Government had a useful precedent in their own recently enacted Poor Law Amendment Act of 1834. When the time came, this law transferred to Ireland with only minor modifications.[23]

The law of 1834 planned to change the existing home or "outdoor" relief to workhouse or "indoor" relief. The cornerstone of Poor Law policy was that families would be broken up once they entered the Workhouse and an individual could not enter or leave without his entire family coming with him. Once inside, the members of the splintered family encountered the unfamiliarity of a highly regimented life behind high prison-like walls, very basic standards of food, clothing and shelter and either the enforced monotony of idleness or irksome work such as stone or bone breaking. It was believed that none but the genuinely destitute would apply for relief under these conditions.

Matters progressed very swiftly in Ireland after the enactment of the 1838 law. Four English Poor Law Commissioners arrived in Ireland in the late autumn of that year. They travelled the country, surveying 94 market towns for their investigations.[24] Eventually 130 Unions were declared - so called because several parishes were united into

Unions for administrative purposes - and more would be declared during the Famine. In the central town of each Union a Workhouse was to be constructed.

An Oxford architect, George Wilkinson, was chosen to design and then superintend the building of all the Workhouses, which accommodated from 300 to 1300 persons.[25] Operating within strict guidelines that the buildings should be of "the cheapest description, compatible with durability",[26] Wilkinson chose rubble masonry for the walls, faced with dressed stone.[27] It proved quite unsuitable to the climate and the walls had to be later dashed or pointed in an effort to combat the ravages of the moist weather.[28]

Fermoy Workhouse
(National Library)

Despite misgivings from Irish M.P.s, the Poor Law was carried by Parliament [29] and George Wilkinson's Elizabethan-Gothic buildings quickly became a feature of mid-nineteenth century Irish townscapes. Asenath Nicholson, an American, described them "upon a pleasant elevation, a building of vast dimensions, tasteful in architecture, surrounded with walls, like the castle or mansion of some lord."[30] Most of them still stand today on the outskirts of towns, solid and unmistakable, their front boundary walls now removed, mirror images of one another.

The Workhouses soon developed an aura of horror and dread, a stigma and a reputation which has scarcely diminished to this day. Much of this arose during the Famine when the Poor Law became the main bulwark in the Government's efforts to deal with the emergency.

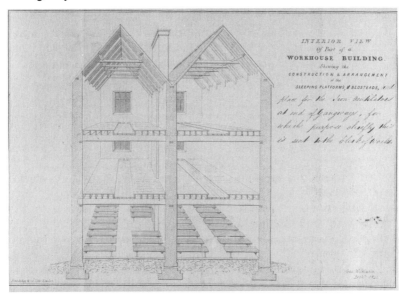

Interior view of Workhouse Building
(Irish Architectural Archive)

Three distinct phases in the operation of the Workhouse system are clear from the records - the few short years before the Famine when everything was new and experimental; the Famine years when the Workhouse system was forced to deal with numbers for which it was never designed to cope; and the long post-Famine period until the setting up of the independent State, when the running of the houses became practiced and routine and numbers fell drastically.

Boards of Guardians were appointed to supervise the orderly working of each Union, under the close superintendence of the Poor Law Commissioners. The Guardians were elected by the local rate-payers i.e. the local property holders who were responsible for financing the Poor Law enterprise. Rates were a new tax and as such, were bitterly resented by those levied and were always difficult to collect. But the fears of the rate-payers that the Workhouse would continue to be flooded by the destitute, as they were in the Famine times, were groundless. Increasingly, apart from the aged, the physically handicapped or the mentally distressed, the majority of inmates were transient, and very few were born and died in institutional pauperism.

The Workhouse world was a private, enclosed and self-contained universe. The exterior face which it presented to the world, in the form of a wall nine to 11 feet high, was forbidding and unwelcoming. The wall surrounded the complex of buildings on all sides and it generally enclosed an area of six to seven acres.

The only official entry or exit to the establishment was through the main gate, manned by the Porter. The name and business of each person was entered on the Porter's Book, with the time of their arrival and departure. Once access had been gained through this gate, one faced the Front Building, the smallest of those on the site. On the ground floor of this building was a large hall, where applicants for relief awaited the assessment of the Guardians on the single day a week when paupers were admitted. There was also a room for the Porter, who had charge of them immediately upon entry, and facilities to have them washed and clothed in Workhouse dress. Here too were the male and female probationary wards, where prospective inmates could be kept in semi-quarantine, if the medical officer so ordered, until admitted to the main body of the house. The inmates could receive visitors on one day of the week for a few specified hours in the front hall of this building.

On the second floor were the Clerk's office and the Board Room, where meetings were held weekly in the most comfortable room in the house.

The Main Building of the Workhouse was 50 yards behind the Front Building. To gain access, one needed to be accompanied by an officer of the house, for internal walls divided the yards and doors were locked. The Master and Matron had apartments in the centre of the Main Building, two rooms on either side of the central hallway. From here they had ready access to the areas of the house for which they were responsible. The men and boys had their accommodation on the right and the women and girls on the left.[31] The workrooms, schoolrooms, nursery and apartments for the aged were on the ground floor and the dormitories were overhead. The yards at the front of the Main Building belonged to the children and the yards at the back to the adults. The sexes were strictly segregated and communication was forbidden between them.[32]

Part of Clonmel Workhouse, opened in 1854 to replace House of
Industry used as a Workhouse during the Famine.
(Courtesy Eamonn Lonergan)

At the rear of the Workhouse site was the Infirmary, consisting of the
Hospital and quarters for "idiots, epileptics and lunatics". They had
their own yards at the back of their building. The Medical Officer had
charge of the Infirmary with the assistance of an Infirmary nurse. In
the early years, routine care of the patients was the responsibility of
pauper nurses. These often came from the ranks of the "separate"
class of women i.e. women with illegitimate children who would not
be leaving the house until their children were grown beyond infancy
at least.[33]

The dining hall joined the Main Building to the Infirmary. This was a
long, narrow room, filled with tables and benches. Children ate three
meals a day here and the adults had two.

In accordance with Workhouse policy, all classes were segregated at
meal times. Before the Famine shattered confidence in the potato,
the diet was based upon potatoes, milk and oatmeal. From the
middle of 1846, potatoes became unusable and then unobtainable.
Indian meal or bread was substituted at the dinner meal, with soup in
winter and milk in summer. In most cases, potatoes did not reappear
as an element in the diet for twenty years and then only at the
insistence of the Commissioners.[34] Meat and fresh vegetables
featured only on the high occasions of Christmas and Easter. The

nature of the food did not require the use of knives and forks. Tin mugs, platters and spoons were the only utensils needed.[35]

Attached to the dining hall were the kitchen, washhouse and laundry.

Until chapels were permitted to be erected in the 1860s, the Dining Hall also served as the centre for Roman Catholic worship on Sundays and holy days. From the 1860s, the Workhouses became more and more Catholic in ethos. In addition to the building of chapels, the Sisters of Mercy came to take charge of the Hospitals in Cashel, Clonmel, Tipperary and Thurles. Furthermore, the schools in Thurles also came under the charge of the Sisters of Mercy in the 1880s.[36]

Two other orders of nuns, the Sisters of St. John of God, and the Poor Servants of the Mother of God, served as nurses and Matrons in Workhouses in several Unions.

Outside the exercise yards was an area for cultivation by the inmates as well as sheds for turf, coal, wool, flax and, in Famine times, for increased accommodation and industrial activity.

Inside the Workhouse, the walls and ceilings were left un-plastered. Instead, they were whitewashed.[37]

Entrance halls, passages, staircases, kitchen and washhouse were flagged.[38] The upper floors were boarded but those on ground level were made of compounded earth or mortar, being cheaper than stone or wood.[39] Such material was considered better adapted "to the habits of the people, most of whom will be without shoes or stockings, and have been accustomed to floors of common earth in their cabins, at a level with, or even below, the surrounding ground".[40] Furthermore, on leaving the house, they would not experience too sudden a change in their living conditions. When Wilkinson returned during the Famine to begin a second phase of Workhouse building, the practice of earthen floors was dropped.[41] New houses or extensions were boarded as a matter of policy, though this practice was much resisted by Boards of Guardians because of the expense involved.[42]

The healthy classes slept in dormitories on the upper floors of the Main Building, but the aged and infirm remained on the ground floor.[43] Except for the latter, individual bedsteads were not provided. Wilkinson devised an arrangement to "combine cleanliness and convenience with comfort".[44] Along each side of the dormitory was a raised wooden platform or continued bedstead, six to eight inches above the level of the floor. A gangway down the middle provided a passage to the door. On this platform were placed straw mattresses or "bed-ticks" which, together with their linen or bedclothes, were folded up during the day.[45]

Asenath Nicholson described "men, women, and children led to their stalls for the night, where are pallets of straw in long rooms (they are sorted and ranged according to sex) to lie down together, with neither light of the sun, moon or candle, till the morning dawns."[46]

The dormitories were inspected every morning by Master and Matron and they were washed or dry-rubbed each day[47] by the female inmates of the house. Single beds were provided only for the old and for patients in the hospital.[48]

Ventilation in a Workhouse was never a simple matter of opening windows, which might too easily be closed again by the paupers in their unsupervised period during the night, when circulation of air was considered most essential. The luxury of fresh air was "little known and less appreciated in the smoky cabins of the country districts"[49] and so a system had to be devised which "cannot be interrupted by the paupers".[50] The dormitory doors were open at the top and they opened onto a central stairwell. Fresh air flowed from open windows high on the central stairwell and into the sleeping quarters. During the day, when the inmates were downstairs, the officers were responsible for the airing of their own areas.

For the greater part of the nineteenth century, sanitation was a primitive matter for all classes, rich and poor. The inhabitants of the towns, in their "congeries of dark, unpaved, filthy, cabin-lined lanes"[51] lived alongside what were virtually running open sewers, with manure pits piled at intervals.[52]

For the large, enclosed community of the Workhouse, sanitation was a pressing concern. Wilkinson compared the Workhouse to the largest military barracks, but without that institution's great open spaces, extended buildings or large expenditure of public money.[53] In the Workhouse he had to devise a system that would be within the bounds of the yard walls of the respective classes.[54]

In each yard was a shed for the privy or "necessary", or latrine. Lime was laid on the floor here and boxes of hay and straw were provided.[55] Charred peat or bog mould proved helpful to absorb gases, lessen odours and facilitate cleaning.[56] Cleaning was done by contract, on a weekly basis but, in cases of urgent necessity, the inmates were put to the task, sometimes earning extra rations as compensation.[57] A drain led from each privy to the cesspool, that "detestable lagoon",[58] situated near the outer wall. This was a deep pit and had to be emptied early each morning, also by contract. The night requirements of the house were met by buckets in the dormitories.[59]

The matter of regular washing and personal hygiene was largely irrelevant to the mass of the population in the nineteenth century, lacking not alone an awareness of the subject but deprived of the requisite facilities of running water, tubs and privacy. In the Workhouse world, hygiene figured prominently in the Regulations, but they were hardly enforced in that crowded setting beyond the cleaning of hands and face in wooden troughs in the washhouse.[60] Even then, the same water and towel was shared among many and soap was in short supply - in the Nenagh Workhouse, the ration was seven pounds to one hundred paupers for a fortnight.[61]

Ruins of Cahirciveen Workhouse
(Courtesy of Adrian Mackey, Author's Collection)

Bedclothes and personal linen had to be washed and changed once a week, according to the Rules.[62] This depended very much upon the time of year, the weather, the amount to be washed, the availability of changes, the number of women fit to do the strenuous laundry work, and the calibre of the matron, whose responsibility it was. Drying and airing clothes was a serious problem, but alleviated when the houses had drying closets erected. All aspects of cleanliness suffered grievously during the chaotic Famine and post-Famine days, when sheer weight of numbers almost broke the entire administrative structure and the health, spirits and capabilities of its personnel. Significant advances were made with the ongoing years with the introduction of bathtubs and the ritual of the weekly bath.[63]

After being allowed entry by the Porter, candidates were interviewed by the Guardians in the lower hall of the Front Building to ensure that they were proper subjects for Workhouse relief i.e. they had to be destitute and have no means of support. Orphans and deserted children could enter the Workhouse unaccompanied, but otherwise the entire family had to enter and leave together.[64] After admission, paupers were registered, examined by the Medical Officer, washed, clothed in regulation dress and removed to that part of the Workhouse assigned to their particular class.[65]

The clothing in which the inmates entered the Workhouse was placed in a bundle and labelled, then placed in the Clothing Store. In many instances, when they came to claim their own clothing on the day of departure, it had simply disintegrated or rotted away in the damp conditions of the store.[66]

Union clothing for women consisted of a cotton dress with cotton or linsey-wolsey petticoat, and a cap and shawl in winter.[67] The evidence from the minute books is that the clothing alternated between periods of raggedness, dirt and neglect and periods of hectic acquisition of new supplies. The advent of a new Matron was the usual spur to action in this regard. In some Unions, for at least some of the time, the clothing was branded.[68]

There was a permanent concern that inmates would abscond in their Workhouse dress. The colours of Workhouse attire may be judged from the materials ordered by the Tipperary house in 1842 - frieze, corduroy, barragon, check, grey linen, linsey-wolsey, grey calico.[69]

The Guardians undertook sporadic inspections of the clothing. In January 1864, in Thurles, they considered that the women "had more clothes than they were allowed" and 210 assorted articles of clothing were taken up - gowns, petticoats, shifts and aprons. The women were noted as having surrendered them only with "great dissatisfaction".[70] Shoes and stockings were provided for adult inmates but children were shod only under pressure from the Commissioners, the Guardians contending that they were not worn by children of rate-payers, except on Sundays.[71]

The gravelled exercise yards were the chief exercise area where "country prospects are exchanged for expansive views of the walls".[72] The children, i.e. those under 15 years, however, left the premises regularly to walk the roads under the care of their teachers.

The Guardians were determined that all able-bodied inmates should be facilitated to leave the Workhouse as soon as they were capable of taking up a position outside. Such a policy meant that the Workhouses increasingly became the domain of the aged and of younger children. In Nenagh, in January 1871, there were 402 registered inmates. Of these, 207 were aged and infirm, 138 were children and only 57 belonged to the able-bodied class.[73]

Workhouse women fell into two categories - the female inmates and the female officers. The inmates were classed in three ways - children (those under 15 years), able bodied and aged or infirm.

The elderly and infirm were not expected to be productive within the Workhouse. Their time alternated between their sleeping quarters and the day room. They participated in mending, sewing, and knitting and, in the more robust days of industrial activity, they engaged, if able, in spinning, plaiting straw, and making straw hats and mats.[74] The elderly women could also be put to minding babies in the nursery while their mothers were otherwise occupied.[75] In clement weather the aged and infirm would take the air in the exercise yard which they shared with the able-bodied women. In some Workhouses, seats were provided so that they might rest in the sunshine.[76]

One of the major breaks in routine for all came at Christmas and Easter. Then all the inmates enjoyed the rare luxury of a breakfast of white bread with tea or coffee and a meat and vegetable dinner.[77] On these occasions, knives and forks were necessary, usually donated for the day by a charitable local worthy.[78] Some of the Guardians generally attended the Christmas meal and a condescending, if well-meant, comment would then appear in the Visitor's Book. In Nenagh, in 1873, Henry Poe wrote that "the paupers appeared cheerful and grateful for the Christmas fare provided for them (beef, slightly salted, potatoes and cabbage.)[79]

With the mellowing of the Workhouse system through the 1860s and 1870s, some houses had Christmas trees and occasional musical entertainments.[80] Kindly local individuals, often the wives and daughters of Guardians, brought sweets, fruit and toys for the children. The old women might be cheered up by a present of a quantity of "genuine snuff."[81]

Able-bodied females came to the Workhouse in various ways. Some arrived with their husbands and children. In these cases, once the husband found employment or simply decided to move on, the entire family went with him. Great numbers came in as "deserted" wives, with or without children. Some of the cases were genuine. In other instances, it was a stratagem which gained the wife and children temporary relief while the husband made do outside.

Unmarried mothers entered the Workhouse to have their babies. These often turned out to be long-stay inmates since they would remain on until the babies were grown. Many able-bodied females came from England and Scotland from where they were forcibly repatriated when, having applied for relief there, the authorities felt that they had not established settlement and therefore the English and Scottish rate payers were not responsible.

In at least one instance, that of Anne Fitzpatrick, the Irish authorities claimed the woman was illegally removed to Ireland. This is her account of what happened to her:

South Dublin Union.

I am thirty-one years of age; I was born at Leeds in England. I never left Leeds until I was about twenty-one years of age, having always resided there in the same house, No. 13, York-street, in Lady-lane parish. I married, about ten years ago, an Irishman, named William Fitzpatrick; he remained living in Leeds for about two years after my marriage, when trade being bad he went to Bradford, where he remained working during the week, but returning to Leeds every Saturday night, and going back to his work on Monday; he continued doing this until his death, at Easter, in the year 1853. After his death I went to live with my aunt in Bradford; after living in Bradford for about a year I was obliged to apply for relief at the Workhouse, which I continued to receive up to the time of my removal.

About a month ago I was told by John Bastow, the Relieving Officer, that I was to be removed to Ireland along with my son, aged nine years; he ordered me to come to his office the following morning where he took down the particulars relating to myself and my deceased husband: about a week after I was brought before the Board, when I was told I would be passed to Ireland; and in another week I was taken by the Relieving Officer's son to Liverpool, and put aboard a steamer sailing to Dublin. On landing in Dublin I went to Mountmellick, where my husband had said he was born, but could find none of his relations there; then I returned to Dublin and was admitted into the South Dublin Workhouse, on 26th November, where I still continue an inmate.

I told both the Relieving Officer and the Board of Guardians at Bradford that I had never been in Ireland during my life, and gave no consent to my removal there, which was done altogether contrary to my wishes and remonstrances. I was not taken before a magistrate previous to my removal, and have no knowledge of any magistrate's warrant for my removal having been issued.

Anne x Fitzpatrick, her mark

Sworn before me this 17th day of December 1855.

Charles S. Crawford, Poor Law Inspector.[82]

The cases of Eliza Bold and Mary Maher, each with three children, received prominent attention in the Commissioners Report of 1857-8. They were both forcibly removed to Ireland, together with their children, from Leeds and Jersey respectively, each having spent eight years in their adopted places. They eventually were received into Roscrea Workhouse.[83]

The case of the deportees Mary Flynn and Kate Cleary was different. They were twice sent back from England and returned each time to Clogheen. Mary Flynn was a widow with three children. She was first deported to Ireland from Birmingham in July 1869. Kate Cleary was a deserted wife with one child who had been repatriated from Chamberwell in August 1869. They remained in Clogheen

Workhouse until 19th July 1871, when they took their discharge. The women and children proceeded to walk to Cork from where they sailed to Cardiff on 27th July. They eventually walked their way through Wales and arrived in Liverpool in late September where they immediately applied for relief. Warrants for their removal from the country were completed on 9th April 1872 and they were deported two days later. The outraged sympathy with which the Guardians usually greeted such arrivals was absent in this case as it was believed that they had applied for relief in England "with the direct object of being deported back home".[84]

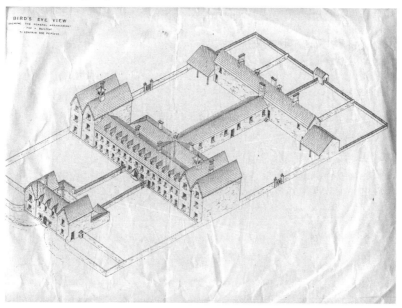

Bird's Eye view of Workhouse Building
(Irish Architectural Archive)

From the authorities' point of view, the least problems arose over the able-bodied females who entered the Workhouse with their husbands and children. Once the man departed, so did his dependents. Occasionally the man absconded, leaving his family behind. Once discovered, the consequences were severe. In August 1848, in Cashel, the family of John Cullen was turned out when his disappearance was noted.[85]

Husbands were sometimes traced to exotic parts of the world. In 1873, the Nenagh Guardians tracked down a Conductor Boyle, then serving with the army in India. They got an initial agreement from the Secretary at the India War Office that 60 rupees per month should be stopped from Boyle's pay both for maintenance purposes in the Workhouse and so that his wife and family could be shipped out to India. But the "revenues of India" were later deemed to be not liable for any such maintenance or transport.[86] In a few cases, it was the wife who traced the recalcitrant husband: in Roscrea, in July 1852, Sally Feeney requested of the Board that she be sent to America with her two children "to her husband, who is in comfortable circumstances and married again".[87]

Discrimination against unmarried mothers was considerable. In Cashel, they were to be "kept strictly by themselves even when at work and when coming to prayer should be accompanied by some of the female officers, put by themselves on separate forms and taken back immediately to their apartments, so that all the inmates can see that there shall be a distinction between those who are well conducted and those who are immoral".[88]

Not all the inmates were cowed by the system. An Ansty Cunningham was cautioned in Tipperary in August 1856 for abusing others and creating a disturbance in the Lock Up Ward. In June 1858, she left the house under threat of prosecution for insubordination in refusing to go to the Lock Up shed. In March 1859, Ansty was back in the house again to have a baby. She went into town for the child's baptism, got drunk and did not return until the following day.[89] The resilience displayed by an Ansty Cunningham was not shared by all those who had to face the reality of an impoverished unwed motherhood. Several babies were subjected to infanticide: other mothers took their discharge from the house, and then abandoned their babies at the gate.[90] Such abandoned, orphaned or foundling infants stood little chance in the Workhouse nursery. The mortality rates were almost total. Of nine such babies received into Clonmel in 1879, eight of them died.[91]

Female children were the source of greatest concern to the Guardians, especially as they approached the years of young adulthood. All Workhouse forces combined with an unremitting determination that the least possible number of children would pass into the adult wards of the Workhouse at the age of fifteen.

For as long as they remained in the Workhouse, the children attended the national school on the premises. Unlike schooling outside until 1896, it was always compulsory for Poor Law children, though the school going population was more transitory. However, from about the age of ten years onwards, there was a concentrated effort to remove parentless children to outside employment. In a rural county like Tipperary, they went largely into domestic or farm service with local farmers.

There was endless abuse and exploitation of the children who had no one to speak for them and who had no proper home to which they could return. Occasionally, however, justice was done by the child. In October 1874, twelve years old Mary Costello went as servant to James Guilfoyle at 10/- a quarter. A year later, she was brought back to Thurles Workhouse by the Master and Guilfoyle was prosecuted for "assault and cruelty" to her. He was fined 10/- for beating and overworking the young girl.[92]

However, the picture is not entirely complete. Other girls displayed spirit and individualism in the face of adverse circumstances and disadvantaged backgrounds. In June 1861, a George Boland had taken two Cashel girls to Anagore Mills in County Clare. They had immediately demanded and received a pay rise. In January 1862, Mr Boland denounced them as "the most ungovernable pair he had ever met who went to sing and make music each night and who insisted that they "be dressed out with hoops and flounces". Their diet was not less than "tea for breakfast, dinner and supper, meat for dinner on Sundays and often besides during the weekdays, potatoes and milk for breakfast". Mr Boland was relieved to report that the girls had now left his service.[93]

A Mrs Woodlock, probably a religious Sister, was the only woman to testify before the 1861 Poor Law Inquiry. She had been "actively engaged in the promotion and management of industrial schools for girls in both Cork and Dublin since 1851." She explained in her evidence that the object of the industrial schools was to train girls from the most destitute class so that they would be able to support themselves on leaving the school. Initially, in the years after the Famine, she had experienced great difficulty in finding girls in the Workhouses fit enough to undertake industrial training, such as laundry work or sewing. When eventually Mrs Woodlock did get some Workhouse girls into her school she found them more difficult to manage and to train than the non-Workhouse girls. She explained:

> At first we intended to make those girls servants, but after examination we gave up the idea, thinking it unwise to send them out as servants, because from their want of information we found them utterly incapable of being useful in any house. They were ignorant of the ordinary things of life; they did not know the names of common objects and household utensils; they could do nothing for themselves; they did not even care to dress themselves properly, and their tempers were so violent that almost a mere reproach brought out that dreadful howl which is peculiar to workhouse girls. We were almost afraid to continue the experiment, fearing to call down upon us public censure in case the noise they made should give rise to the impression that they were ill-treated.[94]

Mrs Lidwell, the Superintendent of Mountjoy Female Convict Prison, reported that the most difficult people she had to deal with were those who had been reared in the South Dublin Union:

> The most difficult class to deal with are the young girls who have either been reared or spent a long period in Workhouses; they seem to be amenable to no persuasion, advice or punishment. When they are corrected, even in the mildest manner, for any breach of regulations, they seem to lose all control of reason - they break the windows of their cells, tear up their bedding, and in many cases (where they have been secured before being able to do any other mischief) they have torn their clothing with their teeth. Their language, while in this state of excitement, is absolutely shocking. They are not at all deficient in intelligence or capacity for better things. They learn quite as quickly, perhaps more quickly than the average prisoners, and when in school are generally very attentive. They seem to me, indeed, to be animated rather by a most perverse tendency to mischief, and a spirit of reckless insubordination, than by love of actual vice.[95]

The Master and Matron of Clifden Workhouse (1910)
("Sláinte" The Journal of Women's National Health Association of
Ireland 1910. Author's Collection)

After a riot in the South Dublin Union the Matron, Mrs Dollard, suspected that some of the young women had stolen clothes from the laundry and directed that the girls should be searched by the female officers. Eliza Dalton told her story.

> I am an inmate of the workhouse 11 years. I think I am now 18 years of age. I was only out of the workhouse three months and three days in that time; I was at a situation that time. I recollect the 7th inst. I was in the hall on that day at breakfast. I saw the women commenced to be searched as they were going out of the hall by ward mistresses O'Connor and Mrs Murphy. The men were standing by about a yard and a half - Maguire and Sullivan- from where the women were searching. The master was standing at the round table and Mr. Foley; Cunningham was letting the women out from their tables. We all began to cheer when we saw the women searches, and that the men would not go away. We said it was a shame for the men to be there. Then Mr. Jenkinson said, "silence, you ruffians, or I will make an example of every one of you" and then I said he dare not do that; and that though we were mendicants and in the South Dublin Workhouse, that we

were not to be treated in so barbarous a manner. He said, "Come out of that" and I refused. He then caught hold of me and dragged me by the bosom of the wrapper; it opened; I had no handkerchief, and my breast was exposed. Mr. Foley commenced to drag another girl, and the master dragged me. I was pulling away from the master, and there was a bucket behind me and I fell over it, and the clothes came over my head. I then got up, and some of the male officers threw me down. I could not tell which of them. I was then held down by Mr. Brady, and prevented from getting up; he held me down by the hands. My hands were over my head, and I could not tell if my dress was disturbed. I knew my dress was up but I could not rightly tell how far. I was crying at the time and Brady let me out. I staid still, sitting on the floor. I was not able to get up, and while I was sitting Mr. Maguire gave me a kick in the back. He first caught me and dragged me as I was sitting on the ground. The girls then gathered round Maguire after he kicked me, and then he left me. The girls then carried me out of the hall bleeding from the mouth, and one arm in my wrapper, the other arm not. The girls then carried me to the corner of the women's yard, and put on my wrapper. Maguire then came at me again. I was sitting down, and the girls round me. I was not able to speak. He (Maguire) reached across to drag me; he did not knock my head against the wall, and Ardina Millar went to save me from him, and he caught her by the hair..... When I was sitting down in the hall, before I was turned out to the yard, Mr. Brady lifted up my clothes, and began to reckon them, and put them down one by one. I had only one petticoat on me.[96]

A philosophy of work and industry permeated the Poor Law system. The most physically demanding work was the washing of sheets and blankets. In February 1870, after a complaint about dirty bed linen, Matron Margaret O'Shea of Clogheen had to organise the washing of 164 sheets and 164 blankets. She complained that there was not sufficient coal to keep the drying room hot enough to get them dry.[97] The job most fraught with danger would seem to have been working on the potato or stirabout boiler. There are several instances of persons falling in and either being burned or killed.[98]

Dublin Union
(Dublin Historical Record 1979)

Industrial activity was at its most hectic during the Famine. Spinning, sewing, knitting, carding, weaving, all figured prominently as women's work. Their labour, combined with that of the men and boys, ensured that the Workhouses became self-sufficient in clothing, and more besides, during the years of the Famine. A trade learned in the Workhouse could be the passport to an improved life outside. Catherine Patterson of Thurles was taught weaving while in the house. She went in September 1852 as a teacher of weaving to Grangegorman prison in Dublin. As one of the very few Workhouse inmates to have left a record of herself, she wrote to the Master:

> I never thought I would be so happy, all owing to your kindness. It was a happy day for me the day the mistress sent me to the weaving. You have done a great deal for me ..... I have 10/- a week and the same rations as any of the Matrons. Miss Hayes took a respectable lodging for me convenient to the prison. I

hope I shall go on well. We have but one loom at the moment. My love to Mrs Moylan and all the girls.[99]

Her 10/- a week is worth noting. At this time the schoolmistress in Thurles Union, Margaret Murphy, was earning but £20 a year, but with the addition of rations and apartments. Girls going into farm service were getting 10/- a quarter, while the mill girls in Co. Clare were earning 12/- a quarter.[100]

Capstan Mill
(*The Workhouses of Ireland: the Fate of Ireland's Poor* John O'Connor 1995. Anvil Press)

Most of the Tipperary Workhouses installed a capstan mill during the Famine. Designed by Richard Perrott of Cork, and based upon a ship's capstan (for winding the anchor cable), it was used in the Workhouse for the grinding of corn. The main purpose was to provide tiring, tedious work for able-bodied males who were always potentially more fractious in idleness than were the females. Up to one hundred adults could be employed simultaneously on the mill. In addition, there was the virtuous Victorian satisfaction of the sight of men literally earning their own bread.[101] Despite Poor Law policy that women and children should not be made work at the mill, they were frequently put to the task. In Tipperary, the Guardians defended themselves that there were not sufficient able-bodied men,[102] while in Cashel Matron Bourke reported to the Guardians that she faced insubordination in that the women declared they would rather work on the mill than in the laundry.[103]

The superior female officer of the Workhouse was the Matron. Second in importance was the Schoolmistress, and then there followed the hospital Nurse and any assistants they might have. The lesser female officers were accountable to the Matron, she in turn was answerable to the Master, and the Master appeared at the weekly meetings of the Board of Guardians to give his report.

The officers lived extremely restricted lives. The high walls and locked gate bound the officers no less than the inmates in a semi-prison life, where leisure and privacy were unfamiliar luxuries. The officers were held accountable round the clock for the inmates under their particular charge. They were accommodated on the premises in conditions which became minimally less Spartan as the years progressed.[104] The basic house rations were cooked and eaten in these rooms,[105] so that Workhouse life made one solitary and self-contained. Time off was rationed - in 1880, the Schoolmistress in Roscrea was allowed out two evenings a week, 7pm to 9.30pm and for four hours every second Sunday.[106] The institutionalised and enclosed nature of the establishment, where a handful of officers were cooped up with one another for days, weeks, often years on end, allowed petty spite and vindictiveness to enjoy free rein.

Some couples met and wed while serving on the same staff, in various groupings of officers. Teachers generally married one another, or the Master and Matron, but Mary Jones of Thurles was the wife of the Porter,[107] and Edward O'Donoghue of Tipperary married the Nurse.[108] The arrival of children complicated the picture and placed great strain on the couple. Only young infants might remain in the Workhouse with their officer parents. Once over the age of two, they had to be sent out, either boarding or to relatives, lest they interfere with the management and subordination of the house.[109] When exceptions were made to this rule, it usually involved the children of the Master and Matron only.[110] When just one partner of a marriage was employed in the Workhouse, neither spouse nor children could visit except on strictly specified days.[111]

Despite the restrictions and drawbacks, many officials stayed in Poor Law service for years on end. Miss Anne Leahy arrived in Cashel as Schoolmistress in July 1857. In September 1865, she married the Schoolmaster, James O'Brien, and in March and June 1870 they became Master and Matron of the house.[112]   Other families established virtual dynasties in Workhouse officialdom: the Laffan females of Thurles, a mother and two daughters, served the Workhouse as Matrons and Schoolmistresses, while the husband and father, Thomas Laffan, was a Union rate-collector.[113]

Restricted and confined though the life undoubtedly was, Poor Law employment provided a secure and structured haven for female officers who might otherwise be homeless and unable to maintain themselves.   Staff had to provide nothing for themselves - they received rations, accommodation, and the services of a pauper servant; their washing was done and there was little on which they had to spend their salaries except to outfit themselves with clothing.

The arrival of nuns as staff in Workhouse hospitals led to an improvement in conditions. The first nuns were Sisters of Mercy who started work in Tuam in 1861.[114] In the following years the Mercy nuns served in various hospitals and were joined by the Sisters of St. John of God and the Poor Servants of the Mother of God. The last order came to the Workhouse in Rathdrum, Co. Wicklow on 19th January 1922 when it had just become St. Colman's Hospital, the County Home.

The Sisters who took charge were Sister Bernadette, as Matron, Sisters Richard, Eulalie, Louise, Maunus, Martina and Rufina as nurses. One of the Sisters described the conditions she found when she arrived in Rathdrum:

> We went through every inch of the hospital and house. The Hospital is in the most awful condition, and the patients are the oldest and most uncared for type. My heart sank beyond words when I saw and heard all. The Sisters will want health, courage and the highest degree of sacrifice to face the work especially in the Hospital part, fancy 190 inmates (20 babies under 3 years, 20 Epileptics, and lunatics) without hot water, very little cold - no lavatories, except for two out in the yard someplace and those out of order - nearly everything is out of order. I am writing this on top of a box, with a paraffin lamp lighted. All are to be on duty in the morning (19th January 1922). I cannot describe how we fared this morning.[115]

Chapter Five: Between the Walls

With the hindsight of a century of social thinking, it is easy to be critical of the Poor Law system, but it must be recognised that the Workhouses performed vital and novel functions in their day. In the one complex of buildings, manned by skeleton staffs, they served as hospitals, orphanages, old people's homes, homes for the mentally and physically handicapped, maternity units, schools, and general refuges for those who found themselves in emergency situations, either long- or short-term. Furthermore, the Workhouse system represented the first awakening of Government concern about the private misfortunes of its humblest citizens.

Chapter Six
Industrious Women

The Lace-Makers

If women had a craft or a skill, it would sometimes protect them from the stringencies of famine, emigration or the Workhouse.

For over one hundred years lace-makers were an important part of the Irish economy. In the late eighteenth century, two kinds of lace, bobbin (also called pillow) lace and needlepoint were made in Dublin and in scattered areas throughout the country, including Cork, Queen's County (Laois) and Wexford. Bobbin lace continued to be made in the nineteenth century and descriptions of the girls at work have survived. In his book, After Sixty Years, Shan Bullock tells of lace-making in Fermanagh in the 1840s:

> In that room a party of young women used to meet to make pillow-lace. They sat on the floor in a circle, each worker with a bottle of water before her to magnify the light from one candle in the centre and as they worked, they sang songs or hymns, or somebody read the Bible to them."[116]

The catalogue of the Dublin International Exhibition of 1865 describes the efforts of Mrs St. George to teach her tenants at Headford in County Galway to be industrious. She established a school for the instruction of girls in pillow-lace making which, she said,

> changed the social condition of the inhabitants of the hamlet so that the people became remarkable for their industry, forethought, and neatness. The prosperity of the place increased; merchants, travellers visited it to buy the lace and leave extensive orders; huts gave way to comfortable cottages and large well stocked shops were opened to supply the wants of the people. The writer of the article passed through the town in the autumn of 1845 when it was like a hive of bees in summer, full of joy and activity and the hum and noise

of industry. At some of the cottage doors were groups of neatly-dressed young girls, seated on low stools, their lace pillows on their laps; and while their fingers moved rapidly through the maze of bobbins, their voices filled the air, if not with melody, at least with heart music. A young mother was seated within the doorway, her foot moving the cradle while her fingers plied their busy task.[117]

These Fermanagh and Headford industries were relatively small undertakings but the invention of a machine to make net in the early nineteenth century opened up a whole new industry to Irish women and gave employment to thousands. Carrickmacross and Limerick lace are both a form of embroidery on net and these two types gave employment to women who would have had no other possibility of making a living. The early machines could make only plain net so that women who could embroider or appliqué designs on the net could add to its value.

Carrickmacross Lace Parasol Cover
(A Renascence of the Irish Art of Lacemaking. Cole. 1888)

Chapter Six: Industrious Women

Carrickmacross lace was made as early as 1823 and Limerick started six years later but, whereas the former was a small cottage industry set up by Mrs Grey Porter, the wife of the Church of Ireland Rector of Donaghmoyne, near Carrickmacross, Limerick-lace making was a large factory-centred industry started by an Englishman, Charles Walker, using capital of £20,000 (some €1,460,000 today).[118]

The first factory in Limerick was set up in Mount Kennet, on the riverside. According to one account it was "a large building with spacious rooms and afforded ample accommodation for the workers which at that time numbered about five hundred". To get a place in the factory was quite difficult. Each girl had to provide a certificate from a doctor, as well as giving her age which was to be between eleven and fourteen years. A reference from some influential citizen had also to be provided. One worked from 6 a.m. to 6 p.m. with the usual breakfast and dinner hours.[119]

Two of the names of early workers are Marianne Hartigan, who "designed from natural flowers and fruit", and Kate O'Brien, who spent the first 2s.6d. she earned on a doll.[120]

The number employed by Walker was very high and several other factories were opened. Mr. and Mrs Samuel Hall, who toured Ireland in 1838, 1840 and 1853, published an account of their travels which included valuable information on lace-makers' lives. They reported that Walker employed 1,100 females, about 800 of whom were apprentices working in the factories at Limerick and Kilrush; while about 300 were employed at their own homes in Counties Limerick and Clare. In all almost 3,000 workers were reported in the area.

The Halls described the different occupations as "tambourers, runners, darners, menders, washers, finishers, framers, muslin-embroiderers, and lace open-workers". The ages of the workers then varied from eight to thirty years. Presumably, after thirty their eye-sight was no longer good enough for fine work.

In the 1840s the children trained for seven years and girls worked on calico for three to six months. Conditions must have been rather crowded: 300 girls were reported to work in one room under a Mrs Blake. Women were quoted as earning as much as 15s to 20s per week by working until 12.00 at night (in 1847, at the height of the Famine). Lace skirts and sprigged net for bodices were made by two sets of workers, one lot outlining the design and the other filling in the spaces with darning stitches.[121]

Kenmare Nuns making Lace
(Courtesy of the Poor Clare Convent, Kenmare)

In their tours taken in 1838 and 1840, the Halls noted "the utmost attention is paid to the social and moral condition of the workers; and good habits are studiously taught them as well as their business; they are remarkably clean and well ordered; and their appearance is healthy and comfortable. Their health is carefully watched by medical practitioners, who attend upon them in their houses in cases of illness, the expense of which is defrayed by the masters".

After Charles Walker's death in 1843 the industry declined and some of his best workers returned to England, but significant numbers remained employed, as can be seen in the catalogue of the Dublin Exhibition of 1853, which mentioned fifteen hundred workers and that the firm of Lambert and Bury did a "large export business".

Other lace workers in Limerick were at the Good Shepherd Convent. The nuns there wanted to find an occupation for the "penitents", as the unmarried mothers and ex-prostitutes housed in the convent were euphemistically called, who were not strong enough to work in the laundry. The Mother Superior, Madame de Beligand, arranged with the Order's convents in Belgium to procure a teacher of bobbin lace. Amelie van Verevenhaven, an expert in Valencienne lace, came to teach at the Limerick Convent; she later became a member

94

of the community there taking the name of Sister Marie de Ste. Philomene. The Convent produced high quality bobbin lace, which was exhibited at the Dublin Exhibition of 1853 and continued to be made there until the nuns changed to making the traditional Limerick lace embroidery on net about 1880.[122]

The most important figure in the revival of Limerick lace-making was Florence Arnold Forster, who came to Limerick as the bride of the Hon. Robert O'Brien in 1883. She was the niece and adopted daughter of William Forster, then Chief Secretary for Ireland, and had lived with his family in the Chief Secretary's lodge, in the Phoenix Park in Dublin (now the residence of the American Ambassador), so she was familiar with Ireland. She was very artistic and had studied drawing in London with several well-known teachers.[123]

The quality of the lace then made in Limerick was very poor. Florence realised that with better materials and design a revival in the industry was possible. The difficulties which the lace workers had to contend with are very well illustrated by Florence's description of her group of lace workers in 1886.

> These workers enter with the greatest intelligence into the idea of a new design, which we used to examine together before it was worked, either at my own house, or in their own little rooms - rooms often so dark and dingy in the most dilapidated quarter of the so-called "English town" of Limerick, that it was a wonder how the lace could emerge, as it generally did, as clean and fresh as if made in the most well-appointed and roomy factory. Sometimes I am bound to say, there were difficulties peculiar to cottage industries. Turf smoke in excess, a drunken husband, and once a cat that jumped through a beautiful "run lace" flounce, when in the frame, to the bitter disappointment of both the worker and myself.[124]

Much Limerick-style lace was made in convents all over Ireland in the latter half of the nineteenth century and up to World War 1. Kinsale Convent of Mercy was one of the earliest and largest centres. In 1847, "looms were introduced into Kinsale Convent for the manufacture of lace and muslin embroidery", to quote from the Convent annals. Rev. Mother Francis Bridgeman procured the services of an experienced lace-maker from Limerick and the Board of National Education sent a qualified teacher to teach the embroidery. We will meet Mother Bridgeman later in the context of her role as head of the nursing sisters during the Crimean War.

In 1848, an "Industrial School" was opened in Kinsale in which employment in various kinds of needlework commenced. The girls who were to learn the lace-making were "bound" as apprentices for three years with their parents consent.[125]

The Kinsale Convent continued to make lace and to provide classes in design. In 1892 Cecilia Keyes, who had been brought up in the convent, obtained a scholarship to the South Kensington School of Art in London and returned to become a well-known designer at the convent. As many as 140 girls were employed in Kinsale in 1909 but the number varied according to the demand.[126]

Lace-makers of this period sometimes got the opportunity to travel to Exhibitions where the lace was being sold. Probably the longest journey was to the Chicago Fair of 1893. The organiser, Lady Aberdeen, whose husband had been Viceroy in 1886 and whose biography is covered later in this book, did much for the promotion of Irish products. She personally chose forty girls who went to demonstrate various crafts at the Fair, including lace-making, and to sell the products. Lady Aberdeen actually guaranteed the girls safety to their mothers![127]

Most Limerick lace at the end of the nineteenth century was made in convent workrooms, where the Sisters of Mercy, the Presentation Sisters, the Sisters of Charity and the Poor Clares tried to provide employment for the large numbers of poor women. Some, like Benada Abbey in Sligo, survived until World War Two because they concentrated on making church work, much of which was exported to Australia.

Chapter Six: Industrious Women

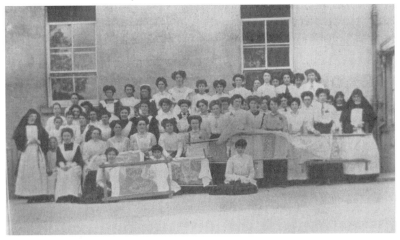

Group of lace-makers, Benada Abbey
(Author's Collection)

Crochet made with a hooked needle and linen, cotton or silk thread also provided thousands of Irish women with a living. The earliest recorded sale of crochet was in the Ursuline Convent in Cork where the children of the Poor School earned money during the Famine.[128] Clones and Cork became the areas where the industry flourished during the next decade. The Adelaide School in Cork employed 120 "young persons of limited means or reduced circumstances." The "difficulty of inducing persons to submit to the discipline and training necessary for the undertaking was extreme and only one applicant in ten was suitable," according to one contemporary source.[129] Cork was described as the "hot-bed of lace" and 20,000 women were said to be employed in the indigenous laces "in the kingdom".

> When men's hands were useless, little girls fingers, by means of this lace work provided for families and, like the widow's cruse, the provision failed not while the famine lasted. One result was the withdrawal of women from domestic occupations. Increased rates of wages failed to induce them to become servants as long as they could procure any sort of a living by needlework.[130]

Mrs Hand, wife of the Rector in Clones, was responsible for a particularly successful crochet industry in Monaghan "enabling 1,500 individuals (at least) in that parish to earn a respectable living." Mrs

Hand encouraged her workers to save but much of the money earned was used to pay for emigration. The importance of the industry to the area can be judged from the comment that "the crochet harvest was only second in importance to the grain crop".[131]

Children in Cork crochet classes were able to earn enough to have their mother and sisters come out of the Workhouse and they all became workers in the crochet trade: the mother would become a "washer", one daughter a "pinner and tacker" and the other two would make "bits" and "barred" (the bars that joined together the individual motifs). [132]

Two descriptions survive of the fate of girls who worked at crochet and are contained in an 1865 publication, "The Lacemakers", by Louisa Ann Meredith.

Ellen Harrington, the young niece of the wife of the Rev. Mr. Longwood, Curate of the Church of Ireland in the village of C., was the only person not a victim of famine fever in the Rectory when the relief ship under Lieut. Hartley arrived with food supplies during the Famine. Hartley described the Rectory as being "originally handsome and extensive" but now "sadly dilapidated and neglected" with "many closed windows, looked like a sick man composing himself to sleep through its decay".[133]

The local doctor, Tom Neligan, gave Mr. Hartley a "talking to", because the relief ship had brought meal instead of bread. When the relief ship returned with further supplies, the Rev. Longwood had also died and Ellen Harrington was living with the family of the Church Clerk who was also the parish school-master. "The school had been turned into a depot for relief stores, and an office for providing Government employment, for any that could or would take it."

When Mr. Hartley entered the room in which the juvenile assembly was usually held, he was for some seconds overpowered by the fetid exhalation from the inmates, which filled the whole apartment, and rendered the atmosphere noxious.

> At a small table in the centre of the room sat Ellen Harrington, so busily engaged that Mr. Hartley had full time to observe the whole picture, which was presented by the room and its curious collection of children, before she noticed him. A heap of cotton-thread was before

her, which she was dividing into skeins, and next it rose a pile of little balls, and a lot of small calico-bags. Standing round her was a group of youngsters, boys and girls, some winding cotton, some holding skeins, and some waiting, anxious for their turn to begin similar work. Every face in the school beamed with eager interest and curiosity, and every eye watched the new occupation, with all the zest of childhood, and all the peculiar intelligence of the bright vivacious race to which these little ones belonged. At length the girl became aware of the presence of a stranger, and she rose, and was deeply affected on perceiving that it was the friend who had been so strangely provided in the hour of her bereavement. With a dignity and self-control beyond her years, Ellen soon conquered the burst of natural emotion that seized her at the sight of Mr. Hartley; and she was able to give him an account of all that had occurred since he was last at C.[134]

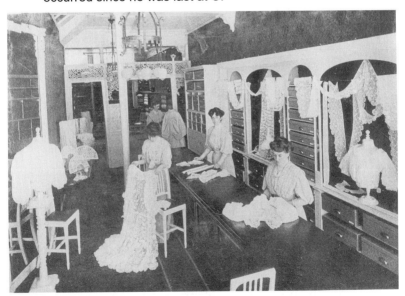

Interior of Irish Lace Depot, Grafton Street, Dublin
(Souvenir Album presented to Lord and Lady Aberdeen. Privately Published. Author's Collection)

Hardship and High Living

Ellen was determined to accept no help from her aunt's family and to be self-dependent in the future. She told Mr. Hartley:

> See, I've begun already, and you've helped me; with some of your five pounds I bought this cotton, and I'm about to get the children to make it up into crochet-edgings, for which I am to pay them so much for every dozen yards; and then I am to send the edgings to Cork, to a lady there, who will sell them for me in England, charging a little more than I pay the girls, as a profit for me: so that, if I have a deal of work, I shall have a large gain, and get quite rich, and the poor children will be earning a living! Is not that good? I'm so very glad to have a chance of supporting myself, and of helping many![135]

From time to time, good orders for laces came from friends, interested through Mr. Hartley's kind mention of the effort that was being made; and he maintained a regular intercourse, by letter, with the industrious mistress of the crochet school at C.

Dr. Neligan also became a lace merchant. He emigrated to the United States because

> I got enough of being doctor, cook, and undertaker to the lot, and won't stay to bury the second batch. There's nothing for it but to cut and run, while my own shoes are whole. Four parsons, three priests, six magistrates, and a score of policemen have dropped through; and only that I have nine lives, I'd have laid my bones in that same charnel house.[136]

Dr. Neligan had great success in disposing of the lace. The export of Irish lace to America became "a very important matter from that time forward. Some £4,000 per annum was said to have been paid to different schools by this one dealer and ex-physician, who embarked impromptu in the trade!"[137] The doctor later went to live in Australia.

Ellen Harrington went on to study at the Ladies Industrial School in Dublin, where about twenty four girls learned to make pillow lace in the Valenciennes, Maltese and English style. Ellen was one of the best pupils, and she was especially good at designing. When the school closed she was sent to the Kensington School of Art in London. Her progress there was highly satisfactory; she became "an artist and a lady, in the true sense of both words. Her drawing entitled her to certificates of merit, and allowances of money, which gave her means to pursue her student life."

Ellen supplemented her income by giving drawing lessons but "she had few acquaintances in the wide, wide world of London, and no sympathisers." According to Meredith's account, "her Irish friends were not surprised when she wrote to them to say that she had a wish to go to the colonies, under Miss Rye's protection; and they prepared to enable her to do so as comfortably as possible. The arrangements for her voyage to New Zealand were nearly completed, and she had written affectionate farewells to all to whom her heart owed them, when an event occurred that changed the whole current of her feelings". She was seen on a bus by Dr. Neligan, in London from Australia to visit the 1862 Exhibition. He followed her to the emigration centre and renewed her acquaintance. They were married shortly afterwards and Ellen returned to Australia with him.[138]

Limerick Lace School, 1907
(Veronica Rowes Collection

Another lace-maker, Mary Desmond, had a less fortunate fate. Mary, the "beau ideal" of Irish beauty, was sixteen when she made her debut at the Carriginis lace school. Her performance with the crochet needle, when her skill was at its height, was incredible and she became the regular model "bit" maker of the school. When a new design was required, it was she who was usually selected to plan the scrolls, foliage, flowers etc. She earned as much as ten shillings a week and grew to be a very handsome woman.

Stole in Tambour, made at the Mercy Convent, Dunmore East
(Author's Collection)

Unfortunately, Mary was deceived into believing that she went through a form of marriage with a man in a higher station in life. She bore him a child and when she discovered that she had been duped , refused to disclose the man's name. She ended her days in a Magdalen Home (a home for "fallen women").[139]

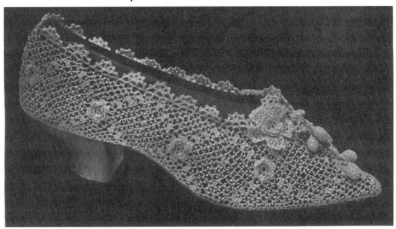

Evening or Boudoir shoe in Irish Crochet.
(Handbook of Practical Instruction in Irish Crochet. The Northern
School of Art Needlework, Manchester. C.1900)

The Congested Districts Board, set up by the British Government in 1891 to improve conditions in the West and South of Ireland, was responsible for the spread of Limerick, Carrickmacross, needlepoint and crochet lace-making to very remote areas. It is not possible to estimate how much lace was made in each style but the industry as a whole was very important to the economy until World War 1. Some of the aid given by the Board was to convents like Benada in Sligo and the Foxford tweed industry, but much of its work for women was in remote rural areas. Lace schools were started at first in the poorest districts where, in a good year, families barely subsisted from their holdings, and where, in a bad year, the people had to be fed by public charity or by earnings at Relief Works. In such impoverished districts, girls crowded into the Lace Schools and worked with unceasing industry.[140]

The most successful school was in Aghoos or Pullatomas in the barony of Erris, County Mayo, which was described by the Congested Districts Board inspectors as the poorest in all Ireland, taking as a test the cash earnings of families and the amount of food raised and consumed on the holdings. Hundreds of families had cash receipts of less than £10 per year. The Board paid girls three pence (old money) a day for three months to encourage the beginners; the girls were so unaccustomed to paid employment that they preferred this steady daily payment to the chance of earning three shillings a week by their industry.[141]

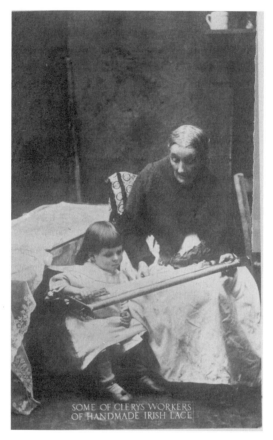

Some of Clery's workers of Lace
(Undated post card. Author's Collection)

The long distances travelled on foot to the schools were only one difficulty the lace-makers had to contend with. Those who were accustomed to working in the fields, saving turf or harvesting sea-weed, had hands that were too hardened for fine work.[142] Girls who were recruited at seventeen were considered by the Board too old. The Board did not take girls under the age of fourteen and girls were refused employment when their younger brothers and sisters did not attend school.[143]   Another difficulty quoted was that in the area of Carna, County Galway, girls would not stay at home in Ireland because, while they did so, their parents got all their earnings "in accordance with Irish custom". [144]

In districts like Pullathomas, Co. Mayo, where no public opinion about industry existed, and where no one was aware of results possible from steady work, workers who earned 10s. a week offered an example to others, and so formed public opinion.[145]   The £1,750 earned by the Pullathomas class in 1906 must have added considerably to the prosperity of the area. The same year the fifty three classes established by the Board earned £21,580; Mayo earnings were the largest, £10,197. It was claimed that "when large earnings were made in lace and crochet the people were able to live in comparative comfort, and out of the girls savings to purchase sufficient cattle, sheep and pigs to stock fully their holdings and the mountains and moors over which they had grazing rights" [146]   Very often the money was saved to pay passages to America. Photos taken of girls from Lace Schools with Lady Aberdeen, the wife of the Lord Lieutenant, who took a special interest in promoting Irish lace, show them to have been well-dressed and wearing shoes; presumably they were all in their best for the photographer who must have been a curiosity in remote areas like Doohooma in County Mayo.

The success of the classes depended totally on the teachers, who also acted as managers and who had to provide outlets for the goods produced and be responsible for the procuring of patterns and thread; also for dispatching the finished goods by post. As each school employed a teacher, their influence must have been considerable in producing the improved standards quoted in various accounts of the girls' appearance. Teachers in Donegal were paid £1 to £1.10 per week.[147]

Wherever lace was made in Ireland, it was an industry which gave women work and money when there were few alternatives. The work was considered preferable to being donkey-girls near Lough Mask.[148] In his evidence to the Royal Commission on Congested Districts, Peter O'Malley, who was a justice of the peace in Oughtarard Union, described the poverty in his area and pointed out that some girls working at cottage industries earned more than emigrants saved while in America and lived more comfortably at home than they would in America.[149]

Fan in Kenmare Needlepoint Lace, Late Nineteenth Century.
Designed and Worked at St. Clare's Convent Kenmare
(Courtesy of the St. Clare's Convent Kenmare)

The average for diligent skilled workers at the beginning of the century was 7s.6d. to 10s. per week; many earned 12s. and these girls would have worked on family farms as well and so contributed to the gross family income in two ways. One exceptional girl actually earned a total of £26 in 26 consecutive weeks. Conditions in the Belgian lace industry were similar to Ireland; Belgian hours were probably longer and remuneration less.[150] One final, significant remark made to the Royal Commission on Congestion in 1906 was that money earned by the women at lace-making was better spent than that earned by the men at fishing.[151]

Chapter Seven
The Nun's Story

Irish Sisters of Mercy at the Crimea.

Life for Irish women in religious orders had its own share of privations, particularly when they were sent on service overseas.

A simple first hand account of the appalling conditions under which the Irish nuns lived and worked at the Crimean War is provided by one of them, Sister Aloysius, in her book "Memories of the Crimea" published in 1897. She was one of the group of Irish Sisters of Mercy who set out from their Head House in Baggot Street in Dublin early in December 1854. The Sisters were part of the first group of women ever to act as nurses in the army of the British Empire. They regarded their task as a mission and were thus deeply committed to it.

The Crimean War (1854-56) was waged by Britain, France and Turkey against Russia and was fought mainly on the Crimean Peninsula on the northern shore of the Black Sea, 300 miles across the sea from Constantinople and from the first hospitals of the war at Scutari and Koulali. About one third of the British army were Irish and three quarters of those who perished in the war died from illness.

The first major battle, at the Alma, was a defeat for the Russians but the allies suffered very heavy losses. The appalling conditions after the battle of the Alma became known in England because the first ever war correspondent, the Irishman W. H. Russell, sent back dispatches to "The Times" newspaper which published on 9th, 12th and 13th October 1854 the information that there were not sufficient surgeons, or dressings, or nurses and there was not even linen to make bandages.[152] The only nursing service provided for soldiers in the British Army at this time was by Army doctors assisted by orderlies.

Russell also reported that:

The worn-out pensioners who were brought as an ambulance corps are totally useless. Here the French are greatly our superiors. Their medical arrangements are extremely good, their surgeons more numerous, and they have also the help of the Sisters of Charity who have accompanied the expedition in incredible numbers. These devoted women make excellent nurses.[153]

On the following day a letter was published in "The Times" demanding angrily "Why have we no Sisters of Charity?[154]

Convent of Mercy, St. Catherine's, Baggot Street, Dublin
(Convent Archives)

As a result of Russell's articles, Sidney Herbert, the Secretary at War, wrote to Florence Nightingale, a wealthy Englishwoman, with connections in Government, inviting her to go to Scutari, on the Bosporus, where the hospitals were located, in command of a party of nurses with the Government's sanction and at the Government's expense.[155] The first party consisted of 14 paid nurses, who had experience of serving in hospitals (there was then no State system of registering nurses) and twenty four members of religious institutions, including ten Roman Catholic nuns, five Sisters of Mercy from their convent at Bermondsey, London, and five Sisters of the Faithful Virgin from an orphanage in Norwood, all under Miss Nightingale's control.[156] Their Superior was Rev. Mother Clare Moore, an Irishwoman, better known as "Rev. Mother Bermondsey".

The Nightingale party left London on 21st October 1854; met up with the Bermondsey nuns who were already in Paris and proceeded to the Crimea.[157]

Sister Aloysius
(Courtesy of Sister M. De Lourdes Fahy)

The Government then decided to organise a second band of nurses and it was in this group that the fifteen Irish Sisters of Mercy proceeded to the Crimea. An appeal was made by Dr. Yore, the Vicar General in Dublin, to the Head House of the Sisters of Mercy at Baggot Street, Dublin for volunteers. Letters were sent from there to the larger convents. The final party is listed in a memorial tablet in the Convent of Mercy, Gort, County Galway : Sisters M. Agnes Whitty and M. Elizabeth Hersey, Baggot St.; Sisters M. Paula Rice and Aloysia Hurley, Cork; Sisters M. Joseph Croke and M. Clare Lalor, Charleville; Sisters Aloysius Doyle and M. Stanislaus Heyfron, Carlow; Sisters M. Elizabeth Butler, Winifred Sprey and Magdalen Alcock, Liverpool; Sister M. Bernard Dixon, Chelsea; and from Kinsale, Mother M. Francis Bridgeman, Sister M. Joseph Lynch and Sister M. Clare Keane.[158]

The leader of the group was Rev. Mother Francis Bridgeman from Kinsale, the most influential figure in the history of the nuns' ministrations at the Crimean war. Mother Bridgeman, sometimes referred to as Mrs Bridgeman, the title given to nuns in charge of nineteenth century religious institutions, came from a prosperous Limerick background and was related to Daniel O'Connell. Even before she entered the Sisters of Mercy, where she took the name Francis, Joanna Bridgeman had experience in nursing as a volunteer during the Cholera epidemic in Limerick in 1832, where she planned her own system of treating cholera – this she later introduced to the Crimean hospitals. She entered the Mercy Order in Limerick, where she was engaged in teaching, nursing and visiting the sick. When she was transferred to Kinsale, she established a dispensary and later an industrial school. Mother Bridgeman's attempts to combat poverty in Kinsale included the introduction of plain and ornamental sewing, net-making for the local fishermen, hair work, muslin embroidery and lace-making. Mother Bridgeman was also responsible for the introduction of nuns as nurses in the local Workhouse during a cholera epidemic in 1849.[159]

The fact that the nuns came from various convents might have been expected to cause dissent but this was not the case. Sister M. Aloysius described being introduced to "our Eastern Mother---- a fine warm-hearted woman. I loved her the minute I saw her. Last night I prayed that I might like her, and that she might like me and I think my prayer was granted."[160]

Sister Aloysius (1820-1908) was the daughter of John and Mary Doyle of Old Kilcullen, County Kildare. She entered St. Leo's Convent in Carlow on 30th April 1849 and remained there until 1857 except for the period she spent at the Crimea. The community Annals describe her as being "a lady of such intelligence and ability, who had a kind heart and an intense love of the poor".[161]

The second party of nuns were usually called the "Kinsale nuns", presumably because of Mother Bridgeman's capability and strong personality. They had more time than the first party to prepare for their journey and their "glorious mission." When most of the group assembled at the parent house in Baggot Street, Dublin, their supplies included soap, starch, smoothing irons and a medicine chest as well as "no end of warm clothing".[162]

The nuns had a very rough passage from Dublin and they were very sick.[163] They spent one night in London and on 2nd December left there with the other members of their group, nine lady helpers and twenty two paid nurses. The "ladies" included the author Fanny Taylor and Mary Stanley, who was a friend of Florence Nightingale and the sister of the Church of England Dean of Westminster.

Sister Aloysius provides an amusing description of the party.

> The ladies and paid nurses wore the same costume, and a very ugly one it was. It seemed to be contract work, and all the same size, so that the ladies who were tall had short dresses and the ladies who were small had long dresses. They consisted of grey tweed wrappers, worsted jackets, white caps, and short woollen cloaks and, to conclude, a frightful scarf of brown holland, embroidered with the words, "Scutari Hospital". That the ladies could be found to walk in such a costume was certainly a triumph of grace over nature.[164]

The sense of humour that Sister Aloysius showed here must have stood to her when she came to deal with the frightful conditions later.

The nuns were themselves an oddity on the train journey across France because they travelled in their veils; all the French veiled nuns were cloistered.[165] The party spent a weekend in Paris; then travelled by train to Lyons and then by steamer down the Rhone to Valence. There, their boat stuck on a sand-bank so that they did not arrive in Marseilles until 6th December.[166] It is doubtful if any of the nuns had ever travelled so far before. One of the Liverpool sisters, a bad traveller, and somewhat advanced in years, thought they had already arrived in the Crimea![167]

Map of the Crimea

The first signs of dissention in the party began to appear. The hired nurses were proving true to type, nursing being at this period a very lowly regarded occupation. They were querulous, vulgar, insubordinate, and not a few suggested an immediate return to England. Their "kerb-stone English" was a source of mortification to their "lady companions"; they were rudely disrespectful to the Sisters; their table manners were appalling and their general demeanour such that the waiters in the French hotels wrote them off as "a set of wild animals from whom anything might be expected".[168] It came out later that most of them drank and that, for many, their reason for going to the Crimea was to acquire husbands.

On the afternoon of 7th December the party embarked on the Egyptus, a rickety unseaworthy mail-boat. Apart from the nurses, it was transporting between two and three hundred French troops to the Crimea. The ladies in the party still managed to acquire cabins, but Mother Bridgeman and her Sisters had to travel steerage in the fore cabins with the nurses. They were also expected to dine together with the soldiers. It must have all been a rude awakening: one evening, after a drunken brawl, the intoxicated nurses and soldiers had to be removed from the saloon on stretchers.[169]

Chapter Seven: The Nun's Story

On the night of 12th December the Egyptus ran into a violent storm and the Sisters found their berths swamped, their trunks submerged in four feet of water, and their pillows afloat in their flooded cabins.[170]

By now Mother Bridgeman had won the admiration and affection of the lady volunteers and the respect of the hired nurses. A picture of her is presented by Sister Mary Stanislaus Heyfron. "Indeed, anyone would like her. She is so warm-hearted and motherly. Added to this she has the most captivating manner and address--- things not to be despised when one has to make her way and win the good opinion of such high functionaries as the deputies of her Majesty's Government."[171]

When the party finally arrived in Constantinople they got a very cold reception from Florence Nightingale. She claimed that their coming out had been "a gross misunderstanding on the part of the War Office" and that there was neither employment nor accommodation for them in the hospitals.[172]

Miss Nightingale was not popular with the medical authorities at the Crimea, who felt she had been imposed on them by an "unwelcome display of Whitehall officialdom."[173] Clearly she had her own difficulties to contend with, but from the start she made no effort to be on good terms with either Mary Stanley or Mother Bridgeman. She insisted on calling the Rev. Mother "Mother Brickbat", or "Rev. Brickbat."[174]

The first appointment for any of the nuns was a dispatch to send five Sisters to the General Hospital at Scutari, which was described as a "dirty, yellow, square, stone building, surmounted by towers at each angle, the whole structure with its cracked masonry presenting such a picture of dilapidation and neglect that Florence Nightingale on first beholding it was reminded of the inscription at the entrance to Dante's Inferno; "Abandon hope all ye who enter here". As the Sisters climbed the rickety landing stage, they were confronted by a panorama of rubbish-strewn mud. Tin cans, pewter plates, miscellaneous breakages from the hospital littered the quadrangle, in the centre of which an enormous pile of offal told its own story of waste and mismanagement."[175] "An araba-load of coffinless shroudless corpses being carried off for burial" added to the horror. And, finally, there was the "fetid stench from within the hospital which assailed the Sisters while they were some twenty yards from the entrance."[176]

Sister Aloysius describes being shown to their quarters "one little room, not in a very agreeable locality."[177] Her first assignment was to go with Sister Agnes to a store, to sort clothes that had been eaten by the rats; Rev. Mother and Sister M. Elizabeth were sent to another store.

> In a dark, damp, gloomy shed we set to work and did the best we could; but indeed the destruction accomplished by the rats was something wonderful. On the woollen goods they had feasted sumptuously. They were running about us in all directions; we begged of the sergeant to leave the door open that we might make our escape if they attacked us. Our home rats would run if you "hushed" them; but you might hush away and the Scutari rats would not take the least notice.[178]

Cholera was raging so Sister Aloysius and Sister Agnes were soon sent to the cholera wards. Sister Aloysius' account of her first day on the wards makes grim reading.

> Vessels were arriving (at Scutari, from the Crimea, which was almost 300 miles away across the Black Sea) and the orderlies carrying the poor fellows, who, with their wounds and frost-bites, had been tossing about on the Black Sea for two or three days, and sometimes more. Where were they to go? Not an available bed. They were laid on the floor one after another, till the beds were emptied of those dying of cholera and every other disease. Many died immediately after being brought in--their moans would pierce the heart--the taking of them in and out of the vessels must have increased their pain.[179]

> The look of agony in those poor dying faces will never leave my heart. They may well be called "The Martyrs of the Crimea". We went round with hot wine, and relieved them in every way as far as was possible. We went to the Catholic soldiers, took the names of those in immediate danger, that the chaplain might go to them at once. He was there; but it hastened matters for him to get the list of worst cases. The beds were by degrees getting empty. If stretchers were bringing in some from the vessels, others were going out with the dead. We

were able to get the men on the floor to bed; then, of course, we could see after them better.[180]

The cholera was of the very worst type---the attacked men lasted only four or five hours.

Medical personnel today may find the method of dealing with the epidemic very primitive and certainly the success rate was very low. According to Sister Aloysius:

> The usual remedies ordered by the doctors were stuping and poultices of mustard. They were very anxious to try chloroform, but they did not trust any one with it except the Sisters. Rev. Mother was a splendid nurse, and had the most perfect way of doing everything. For instance, the stuping seems such a small thing, but if not properly done it did more harm than good. I will give her way. You have a large tub of boiling water, blankets torn in squares, and a piece of canvas with a running at each end to hold a stick. The blankets were put into the boiling water, lifted out with a tongs and put into the canvas, when an orderly at each end wrung the flannel out so dry that not a drop of water remained, before a preparation of chloroform was sprinkled on it, and it was applied to the stomach. Then followed a spoonful of brandy, and immediately after a small piece of ice, to try to settle the stomach, and finally rubbing with mustard and even with turpentine. Rarely, very rarely, did any remedy succeed. [181]

In a letter written to her convent in Ireland, Sister Aloysius wrote:

> If you could only get one look at this dreadful place it would never leave your mind or heart; but you would be consoled to see the Sisters in the midst of so much suffering. The hospital consists of long corridors, as far as your eye can reach, with beds at each side; and as I write poor fellows, both wounded and frost bitten, lie on the floor. We are in the wards late and early. When we go to our apartment, to get a couple of hours rest, we groan in anguish at the thought of all we leave undone.[182]

The attention paid by the nuns to seeking out Catholic soldiers and getting a chaplain to attend them may have been responsible for the accusation made by Florence Nightingale that they were more interested in the wants of the patients' souls than of their bodies but, from the accounts left by the nuns, it would seem that they were indefatigable workers and stood up to the rigours of the situation better then the "ladies" or the paid nurses.

Even so the nuns had some horrific situations to deal with.

> The poor wounded men brought in out of the vessels were in a dreadful state of dirt; and so weak that whatever cleaning they got had to be done cautiously. Oh, the state of those fine fellows, so worn out with fatigue, so full of vermin! Most or all of them required spoon feeding. We had wine, sago, arrowroot. Indeed, I think there was everything in the stores; but it was so hard to get them. We went every morning with the orderlies to get the wine, brandy, and other things ordered by the doctors: we gave them out according to their directions. The medical officers were kind enough to say they had no one to depend on but the nuns.[183]

Conditions were so bad in the wards that the orderly officer did not go in at night because they were "so filled with pestilence, the air so dreadful that to breathe it might cost him his life".[184] "It was said that the graves were not made deep enough, and that the very air was putrid. There were no coffins, canvas and blankets had to suffice".[185]

Even today, stories of the mismanagement of supplies at the Crimea survive, the classic story being about the cargo of boots which were all left-fitting and the consignment of wooden legs delivered to the army at the rate of four per man.

Sister Aloysius' account confirms the conditions. The men who came from the battle-front had only thin linen suits - no other clothing to keep out the Crimean frost of 1854-55.

> When they were carried in on stretchers, which conveyed so many to their last resting-place, their clothes had to be cut off. In most cases the flesh and clothes were frozen together; and as for the feet, the boots had to be cut off bit by bit--- the flesh coming off with them--many pieces of the flesh I have seen remain

in the boot. Poultices were applied with some oil brushed over them. In the morning, when these were removed --- can I ever forget it-- the sinews and bones were seen to be laid bare. We had surgical instruments; but in almost every case the doctors or staff surgeons were at hand, and removed the diseased flesh as tenderly as they could. As for the toes, you could not recognise them as such. Far far worse and more painful were these than the gun or sword wounds; and what must it have been like where they had both?[186]

Sister Aloysius' account contributes the additional information that the food was very bad - goat's flesh, and something they called mutton, but black, blue and green.[187] Presumably this was the food available to the nuns too.

The accommodation first allotted to the nuns at the General Hospital at Scutari was described as:

a dimly-lit and badly-ventilated garret, immediately under which was an apartment called "Scutari Hall", the stench from which could not be eliminated by even the strongest deodorants, even were such amenities then available. The room was unfit for human occupation; its atmosphere was enough to induce attacks of nausea in all but the healthiest constitutions ... The sole equipment of the nun's room was a bed, knife, spoon, bowl and tin plate for each sister. There was neither table nor chair; meals had to be taken picnic fashion on the floor.[188]

If this was what conditions were like at Scutari, they were no better at the Turkish Barracks at Koulali where the remaining ten Irish sisters were sent to set up a hospital. The first few days were spent "rubbing and scrubbing" to make the wards anything like those of an English hospital.[189] It must have been hectic preparing for the arrival of the first batch of sick and wounded which numbered four hundred and ninety. During the period that the Sisters were in Koulali they had a visit from the Purveyor-in-Chief, Mr. Scott-Robinson, who made a survey of the hospitals there. Nearly all the ladies were ill; the nurses were sick too and had gone home; and it appeared, as he stated, that it was the Sisters who were doing the work of the hospital. He called on Rev. Mother one day and requested to see the nuns' quarters. He expressed surprise that they were so badly housed and got them much better accommodation. He placed entirely at their discretion all the stores, food, and clothing, and told Rev. Mother to act as if the hospital were her own.[190]

This later led to charges of wastefulness by Florence Nightingale and her coterie. There were also differences of opinion between Florence Nightingale and Mother Bridgeman on methods of nursing. Florence did not consider that fever patients needed any care other than food. The nuns were also accused of proselytising.

Ward scene in the Koulali Barrack Hospital, and hut hospitals
(Mercy Convent Archives)

At Scutari no chloroform was available but even at Koulali, where facilities were much better than at Scutari, conditions were grim. Sister Elizabeth wrote of "formidable preparations" for operations going on in her ward. At the end of the ward was a "large table with a white sheet on it. Surgical instruments, splints, bandages, lint, etc., are in readiness on this table". During operations, "a Sister of Mercy, in a stiff white apron, with scissors and surgical instruments at her side", assisted the doctor. Later she could be seen "accompanying the doctor on his rounds, receiving his orders, or holding up a frost-bitten limb for his inspection, which she dresses, binds up and bandages"[191]

What must it have been like for the Sisters of Mercy in their heavy serge habits and stiff coifs in the weather which was "fearfully hot at this time, and insects of all kinds abounded - fleas, flies, bugs, ants, mosquitoes. As for rats, dogs, and donkeys, they were innumerable, and you may imagine how hard it was to get a sleep".[192] Two explosions near the hospital and an earthquake added to their difficulties and must have been very frightening for a group of nuns from quiet Irish convents. Even those who had nursed cholera epidemics at home had never had to contend with these sorts of difficulties.

To make matters worse for the nuns who were still at Scutari, typhus broke out in its worst form. Sister Aloysius' lady companion, Miss Smythe, caught the fever and lived only one week. Sister Aloysius considered that it was hard on these ladies, many of whom had left luxurious homes and were totally unaccustomed to that kind of work, some of them never having seen a dead man before. They often regretted that they had no experience and they leaned on the Sisters in every difficulty. Sisters of Mercy had a novitiate of four and a half years, during which they were exercised in various works of mercy, so that the health of the Sisters withstood the shock under which the health of the ladies sank.[193]

There was considerable rivalry between the various religions in the hospitals. The nuns had some kind friends among the Protestant clergy but others seemed to be watching their every move. Letters had been sent to the War Office accusing the nuns of interfering with the religion of the Protestant soldiers and reminding them that they were only nurses – and that St. Paul said women were not to preach or to teach.[194]

The accounts left by the nuns do not tell how many of the Sisters were nurses, but some of the group were lay-Sisters because when one of the Protestant clergymen asked Rev. Mother where she got her clothes so beautifully made up she told him one of the lay-Sisters did them. Presumably the clergyman was referring to the starched head-gear, the coif and the white front piece or guimp worn by the nuns. Rev. Mother then arranged to have the clergy collars made up for them.[195]

The next assignment for all the Sisters was to Balaklava, on the Crimean peninsula. Here the difficulties were equally bad but different. The main hazard was mud! The sisters were accommodated in a wooden hut "not too closely put together" and up a steep slope.[196] Fifteen or sixteen huts all had patients and had to be reached through a sea of mud.[197] Here too the rats were a terrible problem. In walking to the wards at night, the nuns met the rats in droves. The rats would not even move out of the way. In the Sisters' own hut, the rats scraped under the boards, jumping on to the shelf where the little tin utensils were kept, rattling everything. One night Sister Paula found one licking her forehead - no wonder she had a real horror of them. Sleep was out of the question.[198] It is not surprising that one of the nuns developed cholera. The first victim was Sister Winifred, who became very ill during the night. She was looked after by Rev. Mother who never left her but having received the last rites, Sister Winifred died. Even watching over the corpse at night was a problem as the nuns had to keep the rats from touching the body.[199] After this, one of the Catholic clergy purchased a Russian cat which the nuns kept tied to a chair to chase away the rodents.[200]

The nuns were cheered by the arrival of Father Duffy S.J. from Dublin and life was made easier by the building of a proper stone kitchen where they had a charcoal stove and were able to keep the patients' meals hot. Again there were difficulties in getting supplies out of the stores but "Rev. Mother was all energy where the wants of the sick were concerned and made a great fight with Mr. Fitzgerald, the Deputy Purveyor, till she got what she wanted."[201] There was rain and snow that winter. The climate was so fickle that, after a sunny day the blankets might be frozen at night.[202] Great preparations were made for Christmas, even plum puddings for the orderlies, who had a little money to spare and procured the ingredients. Unfortunately, the rats sucked a hundred eggs in the night and killed the few chickens intended for the celebrations![203]

Pray for the repose of the Souls of the Sisters of Mercy, who volunteered to nurse the sick and wounded Soldiers in the Crimea, in the years 1854 to 1856, under the guidance of Mother Frances Bridgeman, Superior, and Rev. W. Ronan, S.J., Chaplain.

SR. M. AGNES WHITTY, Baggot Street,
Died 14th October, 1876.

SR. M. ELIZABETH HERSEY, Baggot Street,
Died in Brisbane, 17th February, 1901.

MOTHER FRANCES BRIDGEMAN, Kinsale,
Died 11th February, 1888.

SISTER MARY CLARE, Kinsale,
Died 28th May, 1871.

M. M. JOSEPH LYNCH, Kinsale,
Died in America, 19th May, 1898.

SISTER M. ELIZABETH BUTLER, Liverpool,
Died in the Crimea, 23rd February, 1856.

SISTER WINIFRED SPRY, Liverpool,
Died in the Crimea, 20th October, 1855.

SR. M. MAGDALEN ALCOCK, Liverpool,
Died the 25th March, 1887.

SR. M. PAULA RICE, Cork,
Died 1st June, 1857.

SR. M. ALOYSIUS HURLY, Cork,
Died 7th February, 1872.

REV. MOTHER M. JOSEPH CROKE, Charleville
Died 7th November, 1888.

SR. M. CLARE LALER, Charleville,
Died 29th December, 1858.

SR. M. BERNARD DIXON, Chelsea Convent of Mercy,
Died 10th May, in New Zealand.

SISTER M. STANISLAUS, Heyfron, Carlow,
Died 18th April, 1887.

SISTER M. ALOYSIUS DOYLE, Carlow.

Memorial card for the Nuns in Crimea
(Courtesy of Sister M. De Lourdes Fahy)

During the month of January the nuns had many cases of typhus and typhoid to deal with. They stayed on duty during the night as the treatment included giving the patients nourishment every two hours. A report sent by David Fitzgerald, the Deputy-Purveyor, to the War Office on 24th December 1855 stated:

> The superiority of an ordered system is beautifully illustrated in the Sisters of Mercy. One mind appears to move all and their intelligence, delicacy, and conscientiousness invest them with a halo of extreme confidence. The medical officer can safely consign his most critical cases to their hands. Stimulants or opiates ordered every five minutes will be faithfully administered though the five minutes labour were repeated uninterruptedly for a week. The number of the Sisters, without being large, is sufficient to secure for every patient needing it his share of attention: a calm resigned contentedness sits on the features of all, and the soft cares of the woman and the lady breathe placidly throughout.[204]

The next tragedy was the death on 23rd February 1856 of Sister Mary Elizabeth from typhus. The night of her death was a wild one. Storm and wind penetrated the chinks in the hut where she lay, threatening to extinguish the lights, and evoked many a prayer that the death-bed might not be left roofless.[205] To quote Sister Aloysius again "It was awful beyond description to kneel beside her during these hours of her passage and to hear the solemn prayers for the dead and dying mingled with the howling of the winds and the creaking of the frail wooden hut."[206]

By April 1856 peace was being proclaimed and there were fewer patients. However, the doctors wished the nuns to remain on. A new difficulty arose with Florence Nightingale over who was to be in charge in the Balaklava hospital. She had recently been named by the War Office as Superintendent of the Nursing Staff in the East and she then assumed charge of the General Hospital at Balaklava, saying she had directions from the War Office to do so. Up to this point, the Mercy nuns, under Mother Bridgeman, had been in sole charge and Rev. Mother was unwilling to remain on if this arrangement did not continue. The patients were nearly all convalescent so Rev. Mother made up her mind to leave. The journey back must have been the easiest part of the seventeen months the nuns spent away from their convents, but they left behind two of their group, Sisters Mary Elizabeth and M. Winifred, who died on duty and are buried on the hill at Balaklava.[207]

Sister Aloysius included in her book two tributes to Mother Bridgeman. Sir William Codrington, Commander-in-Chief, wrote of "the high esteem in which her services and those of the Sisters were held by all, founded as that opinion was on the experience of the medical officer of the hospitals and of the many patients, both wounded and sick, who, during the fourteen or fifteen months past, had benefited by their care." He also spoke of the nuns "unfailing kindness" and the "gratitude of those who have been the objects of such disinterested attention."[208] Other tributes were from Fanny Taylor that Mother Bridgeman possessed "a skill and judgment in nursing attained by few".[209]

Mother Bridgeman was 41 when she set out for the Crimea and, according to Sister Aloysius, was "richly endowed with the gifts of nature and grace". She continued:

> Her very appearance, her manner, and address, were most attractive, and her mind and talents highly cultivated. But above all, there was a halo of sanctity about her that seemed to have entwined the affections of those who knew her closely around her. All the sisters held her in the same love and veneration- and with all these superior talents she governed more like a Sister than a Superior.[210] ...Her whole anxiety was that we should keep alive the interior spirit, and be as much Religious in our new sphere of action as in our Convent homes. [211]

What happened to the nuns afterwards? Two died in 1857, the year after they returned home, Sister M. Magdalen Alcock and Sister M. Paula Rice. Sister M. Clare Lalor died in Charleville the next year. Sister M. Aloysia Hurley worked in the Mercy Hospital, Cork, until shortly before her death in 1872. Sister M. Clare Keane, who died in 1871, spent the post-war period working in the Workhouse Hospital, Kinsale. Sister M. Stanislaus Heyfron worked in the convent in Carlow until her death in 1887. Sister M. Aloysius, whose diary is quoted here, was sent to Gort in County Galway on 5th November

1857 to found a convent there. From there she founded Ennistymon Convent. She was later given charge of the Workhouse Hospital in Gort. She died there on 10th March 1908. Sister M. Joseph Lynch went on to found convents in America and Sister M. Agnes Whitty was sent to Buenos Aires in 1858 but the climate did not agree with her and she returned to Dublin. She died in the Baggot Street Convent on 1st October 1876 and is buried there.

Two of the Sisters went to the Antipodes, Sister M. Elizabeth Hersey to All Hallows Convent in Brisbane, where she died on 17th February 1901, and Sister Mary Bernard Dixon, who worked among the Maori Tribes in New Zealand. Mother M. Joseph Croke, sister of Archbishop Croke, was Superioress in Charleville, from where nuns went to found convents in Bathurst, Australia and a foundation in Kilmallock. Mother Bridgeman returned to Kinsale where she was alternately Mother Superior and Mistress of Novices for the next thirty years.[212]

The nuns' work received very little recognition from the British Government. Many years later, in 1897, Queen Victoria was "pleased to bestow the decoration of the Royal Red Cross on Sister Aloysius," the only survivor of the Kinsale nuns but Sister Aloysius was then 76 years old and she declined to receive the medal publicly.[213]

Conditions at the Crimea must have been much worse than the nuns could possibly have imagined when they volunteered for service. Apart from the physical discomforts and the difficulties with Florence Nightingale, this was the period of the "No popery" campaign and the bitterness of the Oxford Movement. Florence Nightingale had many personality clashes with other personnel at the Crimea. She showed a definite anti-Irish bias when she asked for "more nuns but not Irish ones".[214] She wrote to her friend Mrs Herbert that "the Revd. Brickbat's conduct has been neither that of a Christian, a gentlewoman, or even a woman".[215]

Chapter Eight
At the Edge of the World

A District Nurse on the Aran Islands.

When Nurse B.M. Hedderman was appointed District Nurse on the Aran Islands in 1903, she approached her new post with all the spirit of a Crusader. She needed to. She was probably the first nurse on the Islands and found it very hard to be accepted. The Dublin doctor who told her "your skill will be wasted on the ocean air" was hardly encouraging but her own account of her life on the Aran Islands shows that she was determined not to be put off.

The book written by her was published in Bristol in 1917.[216] Unfortunately, it fails to provide much personal information about the nurse herself. She does not tell us how old she was when she went to Aran; where she trained as a nurse; what nursing experience she had after training or who her employer was. It is probable that she was either a "Jubilee Nurse", the Order of nurses who treated the poor in their own homes and which was set up to commemorate Queen Victoria's Jubilee, or a "Dudley Nurse", the extension of the scheme organised by Lady Dudley, wife of the Viceroy, for poor areas in the west.

Also missing from her account is exact information about where Nurse Hedderman lived on Aran. She tells us that she spent the first night at the local hotel which was managed by Mr. Costello, but it is not clear which island she was staying on. She also tells us that she spent considerable periods on each island when there was an epidemic there. She mentions "the two islands with which I am associated" so it is probable that she alternated between Inishmaan and Inishere. She also mentions, at one point in her account, sending a telegraph wire for permission to do something so she was not quite as isolated as she would have us believe.

District nurses at this period were often provided with their own cottage. In the West, cottages were built for them by the Congested Districts Board but Nurse Hedderman never mentions having such accommodation. "Sending for the doctor" is mentioned in the book but we are not told if he was on one of the islands or had to be brought from the mainland.

The nurse began her book by telling us that:

> This little work has two aims, one of which is to give professional sisters, and others who may be interested, some idea of the difficulties attached to nursing, and the hardships connected with maternity work, in one of the loneliest and most isolated districts in the West of Ireland: the other, to describe in outline, a few of the customs of the people amongst whom this work must be carried out.

Girls dancing on Aran Island
(National Museum of Ireland)

Chapter Eight: At the Edge of the World

Nurse Hedderman left Dublin for Galway on a chilly afternoon in early spring in 1903. She writes of the boat journey from Galway

> I left in high spirits, but the boat was scarcely an hour under way when the rolling motion produced the usual result, and with the aid of a sea-sick companion I went to the cabin to lie down, feeling that the squandering on this first day of even a small share of my stored vitality would render me unable to cope with the unlooked-for demands upon it later. The prospect of unbounded opportunities for fulfilling my vocation as a nurse, even though it involved responsibility in this inaccessible district, made me happy.
>
> Buoyed up with this hope, rather than from the desire of pecuniary advantages, I valued the appointment of District Nurse. The hope of gain served only to supply the oil, without which, as the proverb says, a lamp cannot burn.
>
> I had heard much of the lofty character, the high moral tone, and natural manners of the Aran Islanders, and I thought that work for them would be an honoured privilege. Their patient struggles with the hardships of so isolated a life would, I hoped, bring to the surface any dormant good in my nature. They would be my silent instructors, my teachers; and they in their turn would appreciate my efforts to help them, in however poor a manner.
>
> Suffering slightly from the illness, I made a quick recovery and hastened on deck.
>
> We had been two hours on the voyage, and I beheld for the first time the Aran group of islands rising up before us like real denizens of the ocean.
>
> As we approached the island of Inishere or South Island, I noticed tiny boats moving towards us with great rapidity, the boatmen plying their oars with wonderful dexterity.
>
> As each crew drew nearer they arranged themselves beside the steamer, which seemed a leviathan in comparison. Confusion reigned for a moment, but with

skill born of practice, each was quickly served and, in turn, extricated again with difficulty.

The Captain placed the mail-bag in the curragh. Another man was attaching labels to fish-boxes placed ready for transport; he was accompanied by others whose garb was quite unlike anything I had ever seen before. It was strange to see feet sandalled in pieces of raw cow-hide. They were coat-less and clad in home-spun woollen material of many hues, with variegated belts from two yards long encircling them all round in the vivid colours of the rainbow. They were exceedingly well-proportioned and muscular, and to quote Cowper

"The learned finger never need explore / Their vigorous pulse."

I gazed as they chatted away, but unfortunately, could not grasp much of what they were saying. The Captain, seeing my embarrassment, came to the rescue, acting as interpreter, explaining why I had come. This announcement sharpened the interest of one amongst them, who instantly became assertive, offering to take me ashore in all the "Bearla" (English language) he could command. He assisted me to alight, and called my attention to the little barque beneath in which he had secured my passage. I descended without fear, though an involuntary chill took hold of me when I had to step in, sharing the berth with one of those already named, a rather boorish lad.

Battling with the oars, they sped o'er the waves with special speed, and to me, as to Coleridge's "Ancient Mariner",

"Sweetly, sweetly, blew the breeze, / On me alone it blew".

We did not glide on, however, as quickly as the Ancient Mariner, for we were deeply freighted. There were tar, nets, straw, groceries, goods of all kinds, and fishing gear and curragh tackle around me; with a ballast representing Guinness & Co; for I regret to say that, unlike the inhabitants of Tristan d'Acunha in the South

Atlantic, some of these people do not use water as their only beverage.

It was a new experience, though not wholly a pleasant one, to find myself so soon hoisted on the surface of the waves. Though not fierce to-day, they lifted me sometimes to a considerable height, and I received occasional dashes of spray. This soaking with sea water, combined with the jolting from side to side, wearied me and I longed to rest.

My arrival at the beach created some little excitement. It was new to see a nurse; half the Island people had that day assembled there, waiting for those who had gone on board to fetch provisions ashore. A few girls were sitting on baskets, and others on the rocks, with their knitting. They watched me with keen curiosity, whispering amongst themselves. My chatelaine especially attracted them, and they appeared to concentrate a large share of attention on my hair, which I wore coiled. They asked if it were false. Shortly after landing it burst upon me that, after all, I was a stranger in a strange island.

Travelling between the three islands was very dangerous. The Middle Island, Inishmaan, was described as "the wildest and most inaccessible of the three", and at that period was little visited by tourists. Nurse Hedderman describes an incident in November 1903.

I was returning from one of my usual visits to the far end of the South Island called the Furmina village, access to which is through a succession of sandhills blown and drifted together for many hundreds of years, and known in Inishere as the plain. The short winter day had already closed when I entered my small and cheerless room, to be informed that a person was waiting outside who wanted me to accompany him to Inishmaan. I was changing my clothes when the landlady rushed in to tell me of the great danger that would be incurred; but I simply hastened my preparations.

My visitor, then unknown to me, spoke in the Gaelic tongue; he mentioned that the sea was high, but assured me there was nothing to fear, as his boatmen were unique in the mastery of the curragh, a frail craft, propelled by paddles. When we arrived at the beach to embark there was pouring rain, and the thundering noise of the rollers across the sound could be heard distinctly, this meaning, as I afterwards discovered, that a landing at Inishmaan that night would be a difficult task. However, being then physically strong, and possessing a good nervous system, I resolved to be brave.

Nurse Hedderman gathered her belongings and secured herself in the curragh as the boatman got the journey underway.

We were soon almost a mile from Inishere. The breakers were beating fiercely against the curragh, dashing on my face with a blinding force which compelled me to keep my eyes shut. Up and down we went while surf was flying about in all directions. I was drenched in ten minutes.

The waves also struck the sides of the boat, which was constantly filling with water, while the men kept bailing it out. Soon I saw Inishmaan for the first time - a mass of rocky cliffs, wild and lonely, and a feeling of suffering and despair came over me when I beheld the terrible strength of the waves, white-capped, and threatening to wreck us on the shore should we attempt to land.

Just then a glimmering light in the distance showed one of the Island women holding a candle - our only beacon on that dark night and in such a perilous moment. It was then after 10 o'clock at night.

We waited a long time in vain to effect a landing, but at length, during the ebbing of a wave, one of the men endeavoured to hold the curragh while the other directed me to get on his back. To this I willingly consented, for tired and wearied, I longed to reach my destination. Suddenly, as we were about to step out, a huge wave struck us. The boatman missed his footing, slipped and stumbled, and we were both plunged to the neck in the merciless torrent.

Chapter Eight: At the Edge of the World

My condition was now hopeless; indeed, one idea alone possessed me, that was a longing desire to return to civilization at the shortest possible notice. After a little time the men came to the rescue, and I was dragged on to the rocks, wet and shivering.

I had then to trudge over a path of limestone rocks, with heights and hollows of so intricate a nature as to be in places almost impassable. The stones were mud-covered, and in this condition had been trodden by the natives for centuries. As we went along, the women chatted in their native tongue, a beautiful and expressive language, which at that time I did not understand.

A forlorn and bedraggled Nurse Hedderman arrived at her patient's cottage, where she was forced to change out of her sodden uniform into a native islander's dress.

A Jubilee Nurse's Cottage
(Aberdeen Souvenir Album. Author's Collection)

Another sick-call proved equally hazardous, as once again she was summoned by a boat-man.

We hurried to the beach, where his curragh lay moored; the night was dark and threatened to be still darker; no stars, no moonlight, but a dim gloom over the sea - a dreaded sight. However, I was too much absorbed in the work before me to take further notice of the forces overhead. My mind was centred on what condition the patient might be in, for I had no hope of medical assistance - this latter was out of the question at such short notice.

As I hastened on board with a box of dressings, heavy clouds could be seen fast gathering, and shadows, up to now unnoticed, were hanging near.

I had implicit confidence in my gondoliers, who were old sailors, having crossed and re-crossed that sound many times, and surely it was not possible for any hidden rock to be unknown to them. Before the curragh had been ten minutes under way, the mist, that had all along hovered over us, now settled down thick and fast, rendering both islands invisible. This necessitated moving slowly, with eyes strained towards our destination, though to reach it appeared at the moment to be absolutely hopeless. One of the crew proposed turning back, but that course was just as dangerous as rowing onwards.

My own position was an unpleasant one - stowed away almost at the bottom of a frail curragh where necessity obliged me to remain, and to exhibit good courage; for alarms serve only to increase the desolation the night had in store. We kept pulling back and forth for a long time and at length rowed into what the men understood to be the middle of the sound, steering for the slip or landing-place at Inishmaan, when suddenly we caught a glimpse of something like a spark flickering some distance away. As we faced it, it seemed to vanish, so that the rowers concluded I had been mistaken, and tried to explain that I had seen only the phosphorescent gleaming on the surface of the waves. Unheeding this, from my cold observatory at the stern I watched for the light to re-appear, which it did, seeming to revolve. I thought it was Inishere lighthouse, but this they declared impossible, informing me at the same time how well qualified they themselves were to navigate between the Islands, even if no land could be discerned.

Chapter Eight: At the Edge of the World

They also related the varied and hazardous perils they had up to then undergone, with little concern as to the effect this unnecessary information might have on their unfortunate passenger.

The haze and darkness combined were now too heavy to admit distinguishing anything at all - the sky and sea seemed one. The boatmen were sure that our advance was towards the Inishmaan side of the sound, and thought that the light glimmering on shore was that from a lantern which one of the natives had taken to meet us, as was their custom when the nurse is sent for on moonless nights.

My own attention was always directed to the shore, hoping for some signal, and as they rowed on with rather increased speed, suddenly one of them shouted with all his might, screaming aloud, 'Seacan'! (Take care). We were on the rocks; and a little point had perforated the boat, and water came rushing in. I understood the situation and shuddered.

We were on the edge of a small chasm, big enough, however, to engulf our frail little craft. There was no time - I was struggling in the water, and trembling with the chill of long exposure.

One of the men stepped out, grasping an oar, trying to feel his way, when an incoming ground wave dashed it from his hands, precipitating the poor fellow almost to the neck in its depths. The other assisted me to a slippery footing, where I had to stand propped against a large boulder to recover from the shock.

Imagine my consternation when it was discovered we were back again in Inishere. There was nothing for it but to stand beside that lonely rock, bewailing the cruel fog which prevented rendering any assistance to the little patient that night. How true was my conjecture! It was Inishere lighthouse!

Travelling by land was also perilous and it was always on foot. At that period there were no roads on the Middle or South Island. Such paths as there were had no camber to drain off water. The loads of seaweed carried long distances from the shore wore away the centre, so that in winter, when mud and water settled in the middle, journeying from one part of the island to the other was very difficult. At the height of the worst storm she had seen on the island, Nurse Hedderman was summoned to a patient. She started out clinging to her guide but they were pushed backwards and forwards every other moment in their attempts to make progress. When they arrived at the patient's cottage, the husband gave the nurse some matches and went in search of his mother. Nurse Hedderman describes the cottage:

> The bleak bare house and its surroundings were very depressing, and I longed for a companion to hand anything I wanted, as the patient's condition was far from normal. I had to exercise all my skill and quickness with her unaided, for it would have been impossible to procure medical or any other help in that storm.

> The only source of light was the few matches and a lamp fuelled by fish oil, "but the task of trimming the apparatus in common use was mystery to me, and I could hardly see the patient, in addition to which the draught coming in through so many holes quickly consumed the few matches. For the law of diffusion was certainly in full operation here. There was ventilation truly in more than abundance! It was a case of groping one's way all the time along a damp wall, which was anything but impervious to the cold.

> When the patient was a little rested, the sudden call was explained to me in Gaelic. She said it was unexpected, and I did the best under the circumstances, though I had to manage with next to nothing; with scarcely enough water to drown an antiseptic tabloid in, and, with the exception of the small articles my little store contained, a scant supply of linen; there was, besides, the inconvenience of having the room shared by two children, a girl of four and another toddling infant who peeped at me, half scared, from beneath the bed-clothes.

Chapter Eight: At the Edge of the World

As I waited patiently, watching for changes incidental to such cases, I could hear the wind raging outside, groaning and whirling on the wooden tarred roof over me. It was dreadful to hear the drumming sound of the storm, straining the rafters almost to breaking point, slamming the door, and rattling the little window in its loose-fitting casement.

After making the poor woman as comfortable as possible, I had to depart homewards. The husband had at length returned, and after fastening my cap and cloak we started, but we had scarcely gone a few paces when the tempest carried away his hat. Trying to keep it on, he let go his grasp on my hand, and directly, a blinding squall lifted me from the ground without any kind of warning, carried me along and deposited me in an excavation about five feet deep, from which stones had been quarried for building purposes long before - a trap we were just trying to avoid. I was stunned, and half hidden with the sand blowing overhead; but fortunately there was no water, and when, at the end of a few awful minutes, I clutched a sand-bank for support and got out, my guide reappeared, much affected at the situation I was in.

I was endowed with supernatural strength for the remainder of the journey and managed to reach my lodgings; but that night brought me no sleep, for the rain which fell in torrents soaked through the roof of my room. At dawn, I saw that some of the houses were thatchless, and reports from all parts, in the days following, confirmed my risky experience of the force of this storm.

In her account, Nurse Hedderman describes a typical day's work when she had been two years on the Island:

My daily work was chiefly visiting the homes and attending maternity cases. Sometimes a climb over the limestone hills, that one met at every turn, was the only means of access to the houses in which the poor live, sometimes the hills of drifted sand had to be surmounted when the east wind blew; and a morning start over the plain was by no means a pleasant task.

On ordinary duty I began to visit my patients about eight o'clock, but this hour varies according to the nature of the case, the distance to be got over, and any other circumstances that may tend to alter the rule, as fixed laws are out of the question in Aran. The elemental forces step in suddenly and sometimes frustrate our most cherished hopes - planning in advance must not be thought of here.

Rising earlier than usual one March morning I found that a strong gale was sweeping over the plain with an almost equatorial violence. I had promised to visit a newly-made mother, because lactation had not been established, and well-meaning neighbours have a habit of giving babies many fearful abominations. I dreaded interference, and had some doubts as to the treatment the baby would receive if entrusted to these ignorant women, so go I must; but what an expanse of sand intervened, though I thanked God it did not necessitate a sea journey that morning. The way was tedious enough and what course to steer perplexing. Looking in the direction of the plain, where the drifting sand was simply blinding, I saw that route was impossible; so glancing cragways, I decided in favour of the latter, though a long stretch of rock separated me from the nearest village, and yet another hill required climbing before my walk would terminate, with the crag-swept blast fierce against me. A short distance away the foaming Atlantic was swelling and tossing, dashing its ruthless waters in reckless fashion on the very rocks beneath my feet - but I was regardless of its seething fury to-day, rage as it would.

Eventually, the nurse fell:

I stepped on a stone that projected from a ledge of rock; but directly I rested my weight upon it, it gave way and I fell with a rebound a considerable distance. I was almost senseless, being pressed against the edge of a stone, and the shaking more intense than the pain. Had a limb been fractured, I should have perished without assistance, for, not being generally used by the Islanders except as an occasional short cut to the shore, the place was so deserted that relief if necessary was not available.

The baby Nurse Hedderman was to visit had been born asphyxiated and was consequently very weak but was found remarkably well.

On another journey Nurse Hedderman was chased by a bull, "a huge monster, roaming wild, who seemed to shake the hedge to its foundations, scattering the earth like chaff at his feet." She continues:

> With a desperate effort I tore off my cloak, flinging it behind me. At this he immediately pulled up, and kept turning and scenting it, while at a bend in the lane a little distance away I entered another field and succeeded in climbing a wall, breathless, panting, and exhausted. I reached the top utterly terrified, and trembling all over. When I recovered a little, I gazed from my perch like a cat in a tree, and beheld the two formidable horns of my pursuer entangled in the holes they had torn in my cloak.

> He held the garment up desperately confused, striking the earth beneath him and evidently seeking to extricate himself. He could see nothing, and was dashing wildly here and there, and in this condition he was found two hours later.

> My cloak was triumphantly returned to me, looking as mangled and mutilated as if it had passed through a siege.

The harsh conditions endured by some islanders are illustrated by Nurse Hedderman's description of the worst cottage on the island:

> The walls in many parts were bulging with moisture, and its every corner spoke of dilapidation. The roof too was in holes for want of sufficient thatch. There was no chimney -- nothing but a few rude boards nailed together in triangular fashion leading to fireplace of solid bare stone. The window was a single pane, quite unmovable, so that very little fresh air ever penetrated

the interior … The one room with its earthen floor, and a loft to which the children ascended by means of a ladder, provided all the space a family of eight could obtain … This cottage was readily distinguished from the more clean and comparatively comfortable dwellings tenanted by the neighbours.

Describing a maternity case, the nurse writes:

Let nurses with aseptic knowledge imagine what it must be to come to a home like this is the early hours of the morning, with a stiff gale blowing, so that medical help was an impossibility. The patient lying on the floor, well-nigh exhausted with P.P.H., no fire or other convenience to hand; water as scarce as wine; no basin or table, but a large stool on which were placed a few mugs; the indispensable kettle coated with fallen soot. Antiseptic precautions indeed!

To add to her troubles, the new mother's husband was mentally defective and wanted to give the patient poteen.

Inishmaan, the Middle Island, is described in winter as "bleak and desolate, bare and weird-looking. It was one of the loneliest places in the world and so little protected from the fierce Atlantic gales that for many months one heard without cessation the deafening roar of that never-resting ocean."

It was, she continues, "inhabited by people entirely different from those met on either of the other islands:

They speak nothing but their native Gaelic, and from earliest childhood are inured to every conceivable hardship, with the result that their power of endurance is greater, strengthened perhaps by the compelling influence of having to earn a livelihood under almost the worst conceivable conditions of soil and climate.

Scattered about the Island, little patches of tillage revealed themselves here and there. These, though small in themselves, furnished wonderful proof of the industry and thrift of the inhabitants. The ground consisted practically of bare stones, covered with sand and clay, carried for generation after generation, from wherever it might be found, not by beasts of burden but

Chapter Eight: At the Edge of the World

on the backs and shoulders of human beings. From this soil the natives of Inishmaan reaped a scanty crop for their harvest and winter store. It is only an indomitable and wonderfully persevering spirit that could extract any return from such flagstones and rocks."

There was no pier worthy of the name on Inishmaan.

Three generations of an Aran Family
(National Museum of Ireland)

Despite all the privations of life on the island, however,

Many can boast of having passed the allotted span. There is no disputing the fact that most of the people are improperly nourished; but one thing is certain - what they eat is deprived of those culinary accessories and mixtures that bring disease to the rich and better fed, and the diet they are obliged to subsist upon is better calculated to promote health. Fish - fresh in the spring and dried at other times- is their chief protein. This is one reason why they are so capable of performing work which to an outsider would be considered impossible.

Women's work on Aran included the harvesting of kelp (seaweed). In Nurse Hedderman's time, it was an almost valueless industry because of the low prices available but she tells us about the labour entailed in its manufacture.

The weed from which it is made is first cut, carried in dripping baskets by people of both sexes, sometimes up cliffs of great height, spread to dry and then stacked. All this takes months working many hours a day. The weed is then burned and this operation entails constant supervision.

Nurse Hedderman believed that the industry added to her work-load, because many chest and kidney diseases on the island were due to the necessity of passing so many hours exposed to the intense heat incurred by this work. "The heavy perspiration given off when stoking the fires predisposed workers to chills when they afterwards returned to the cold atmosphere of their homes."

A boundless belief in fatalism among the islanders made life more difficult for the first nurse. Diseases like scarlet fever, measles, and whooping-cough were regarded as inevitable and "the sooner a child got them the better" was the accepted doctrine. During the whooping-cough epidemic in the spring of 1908, the nurse found it impossible to get mothers to isolate children who were already affected from those who were well. When she visited a house during a scarlet fever epidemic she found "not only relatives at the houses but outside visitors as well, and when remonstrated with they would placidly reply "tis only a cold, Miss, and will walk off the Island." In desperation she wrote that "Pasteur himself would fail in teaching the 'germ theory' here; their own therapeutic remedies are the preventatives par excellence." Local "cures" proved a major difficulty to contend with.

Chapter Eight: At the Edge of the World

There was also a native aversion to doctors, as well as everything associated with medicine in any form. The Dispensary was regarded as a kind of guillotine or death trap - a tribunal from which, if they entered, they were never to emerge. By the time Nurse Hedderman's book was written, most of this hostility had disappeared, but before that, in the early days, nursing work was a very thankless task.

Threshing Corn on Inishmain
(*Glimpses of My Life on Aran*. B.M. Hedderman)

Nurse Hedderman tells us of some of her difficult cases. A poor man with a large family was ill with what she reckoned was an acute attack of Bright's disease. Though she had not been sent for, the nurse called to the patient's house and when she saw the condition he was in, she advised his wife to send for the doctor. She refused to do this, so the nurse set about preparations for a vapour bath and ordered a fire to be lit and a supply of water brought. The wife boldly expressed the opinion that the nurse's treatment could be of no avail because her husband had been looked upon by an "evil eye" one morning on the strand. It turned out that the man had already been treated by the local "witch charm" and the family wanted to wait for it to work before sending for the doctor. Eventually they were forced to get the doctor and the man recovered after a spell in hospital.

On Inishere, particularly, the people did not send for the nurse in time or until local cures had failed. One of the nurse's early patients was a woman who had received a wound, a "loc" in Irish, which had been treated by rubbing dirt into the wound. By the time the nurse was called, there was severe inflammation with severe throbbing, the wound having been treated with a smelly poultice which "would have required the skill of an analyst to detect all its ingredients." The nurse applied a "soothing antiseptic lotion with lint and cotton wool held in place by a bandage", but when she returned the next day the dressing had been removed and the old lady had resorted to someone else's method of cure. This time it was a compound of dock leaves blended with snails. Nurse Hedderman must have been a superb nurse because again the patient recovered!

A child who had whooping-cough developed bronchial pneumonia; when she deteriorated rapidly, the mother was convinced she had been taken by the fairies and that the "good people" had substituted for her child "that object", pointing to the poor little patient on the bed. Later, one of the Island 'Gamps' entered, "a rather clever woman in her own way, and tossing her tangled tresses disdainfully while she watched the nurse's efforts to help the child, said quite audibly, in Gaelic, "Tis little good your cure will do". Again the child recovered, which must have helped Nurse Hedderman's reputation considerably.

Another difficulty was getting people to accept that tuberculosis could be contracted in the limbs. The mother of a boy with a tuberculous knee is reported as saying "Who ever heard of consumption in a person's leg?"

On the two islands where the nurse served, the men's conversion to modern methods was much more pronounced than the women's, except amongst those who were utterly illiterate. The women clung to their ancient beliefs in the supernatural with a tenacity which Nurse Hedderman found hard to credit.

An old man came to the nurse in terrific haste one morning. She knew by the speed with which he announced himself that some catastrophe had occurred. His face looked as confused as if he had taken an opiate. "She drank the bottle," he said breathlessly.

Chapter Eight: At the Edge of the World

Some time before this the nurse had procured a liniment for his wife, but was not aware that it contained any such poisonous ingredients as would cause the symptoms he described. It was a mild terebene preparation - of course marked for external use only. Unfortunately he could not read this for himself. The nurse made haste to the patient's side, and found her "livid and shivering, suffering from violent pains and from what seemed gastro-intestinal irritation. Vomiting was threatened, and we prepared an emetic, thus preventing this puzzling "poison" from doing further harm. No trace could be found of the liniment bottle prescribed a few days before."

Four Generations at Inishmain
(*Glimpses of My Life on Aran*. B.M. Hedderman)

Anyhow, the nurse gave the emetic, and after a short interval it had the desired effect. A fluid mingled with the greenest grass-like substance was vomited, so green-looking that it perplexed and bothered Nurse Hedderman. It was very awkward to question the patient but it was obvious to the nurse that the liniment could not have produced such green mucilage. It turned out that a local woman had a few days previously ordered the patient to chew the greenest leaves of a special shrub that grew by the wall of the cemetery, where this self-constituted doctor had found the patient in the act of exploring or rather desecrating the grave of a long-lost friend in search of a molar tooth, a much vaunted cure for rheumatism.

Another patient in the early days of the nurse's sojourn on Aran was convinced he had a "worm" in his ear. When the nurse syringed the ear "it bore evidence of previous tampering in the hope of expelling the supposed invader, for an abscess was forming. When the ear was washed out again the next morning large masses of septic material came to light, and were evacuated in the form of little crusted pellets; on seeing them the patient exclaimed loudly "The worm, the worm". With daily care the injured ear made a speedy recovery.

Several times Nurse Hedderman complains of the delay in seeking treatment. One young man with a badly inflamed leg, made worse by the constant friction of wet flannels soaked in sea water, came for treatment. When he received a temperance lecture from the nurse before the leg received attention, he quickly replied that the drink could not reach down to his leg! He also informed the nurse that "If Solon and all the preachers lived long in Aran, they'd want a pint". Later, when the same man got an infected finger he was treated to a dissertation on infection. His father blamed the infection on the fact that he had not taken a red coal from the fire on St. John's night, one of the many superstitions supposed to protect from the machinations of the "Evil One".

On another occasion the Nurse tried to persuade a man who suffered from a hernia to go to hospital for surgery. He protested, on the grounds that his brother died from a similar ailment. He did not believe Nurse Hedderman's explanation that his brother had been too slow in seeking advice. The nurse asked the patient if at some time he had overstrained himself. This he dismissed as nonsense claiming that he had been "overlooked" by somebody. The nurse went the nine mile sea journey to procure him a truss only to find on her next visit that he had not even tried it on.

All islanders were superstitious but the fishermen were the worst. A barefooted female met on the way to the boats would force them to return to their homes; meeting a fair or red-haired girl made the men go in the opposite direction.

Nurse Hedderman found the poorest people the most free from superstition. A man was known to level a wall in one of the two rooms he possessed, because he dreamed the night previously that the wall hindered the passage of the "good people", and that this accounted for any ill-luck that had befallen him in the past.

Traditional & Modern dress on the Aran Islands c.1910
(National Museum of Ireland)

To prove that she did not believe in such superstitions, Nurse Hedderman moved house on what was considered a "cross" or unlucky day. Her friends on the island sympathised with her on her approaching misfortune but were disappointed when nothing wrong happened.

There were also many superstitions relating to marriage. One woman refused a very good settlement because it was an autumn offer, protesting that what is bound in that season is loosed in the spring. Most marriages were performed on a Friday, a custom directly opposed to that prevailing on the mainland. The "borrowed plume" at a wedding was usually the ring of some relative or lucky individual. The bride did not enter her parents' home for a month under pain of expulsion but she could sit on the door step and chat across the threshold. One girl, who infringed this rule when her mother became ill, was reputed to be of a feeble cast of mind, something denied by Nurse Hedderman.

According to Nurse Hedderman, "the emotion 'love' was almost unknown amongst the people. Marriage was more a commercial bargain than an affair of the heart; consequently, if there was any tender feeling, it was not outwardly demonstrative and, except in a few cases, affection did not enter into the question of matrimony at all." Everybody married on Aran and married young, which accounted for their ever-increasing families and consequent poverty in the homes.

Nurse Hedderman concluded her account with a stoical appraisal of the role of the district nurse:

> The responsibility of a district nurse in such a spot is truly great, and more exhausting than the heaviest hospital work; and it is difficult to leave the Island for months at a time. It is so wild around the shore that frequently no doctor can venture to land. Therefore, however critical the case nay be, the district nurse must face it alone and unaided and just do the best she can.

Chapter Nine
More Irish than the Irish Themselves

The Lord Lieutenant's Wife

At the other end of the spectrum from Nurse Hedderman and her patients was Lady Aberdeen. Of all the women discussed in these pages, Ishbel Aberdeen was probably the wealthiest, the most politically important, and the one with the strongest social conscience. She was also the only one with an international reputation. Though she was Scottish and spent only ten years in Ireland, her impact on Irish affairs, and especially on Irish womens' lives, was considerable. It could be argued that she did more for Irish women and in a greater variety of fields, than any of her contemporaries.

Ishbel Marjoribanks was born in 1857 in Scotland, where her family had considerable estates. Her childhood was spent between the Scottish estates and London, where the family home was in Mayfair. She had a very strict upbringing and was educated at home and at school in London. In 1875 she was presented at Court and two years later she became engaged to Lord Aberdeen, whose family also owned estates in Scotland. After her marriage, and an extended honeymoon in Egypt, her life for the next eight years was spent, like her childhood, between the Scottish estates and the London social scene. Haddo House was the Aberdeens' main residence in Scotland where they spent the autumn and winter, varied by visits to Ishbel's family properties at Guisachan and Cromar.[217] The Parliamentary season was spent mainly in London, at their house in Grosvenor Square.

The Aberdeens had five children, one of whom died in infancy. They were very improving landlords and tried to make the lives of their staff and the community round them happier. Lady Aberdeen claimed that "in all the British Isles there can be no landlord who had better reason than A. to be proud of his tenants and of the relations existing between him and them".[218]

Lady Aberdeen
(Undated Post Card. Author's Collection)

Lady Aberdeen also held religious classes and social gatherings and was involved in a number of movements in London. The "Upward and Onward" society was originally started for the benefit of farm servant girls on Lord Aberdeen's estates. It extended to improving the morals and working conditions of all their servants and tenants. Eventually the movement spread to other areas of Britain and had 115 branches and a membership of 8,280.

The Aberdeens had a very active social life and were strong supporters of Gladstone. When he became Prime Minister in 1886, he appointed Lord Aberdeen as Viceroy, the king's representative, in Ireland. The Aberdeens arrived in Dublin in February but their term, in office ended the following August because Gladstone was defeated in Parliament and went out of office.

Lady Aberdeen's time in Ireland was very busy. They arrived in Kingstown, now Dun Laoghaire, Dublin, early on the morning of 20h February 1886. Lady Aberdeen was already taking a very active part in the Vice-Regal administration. On her instigation, the Aberdeens' children accompanied their parents on the public journey to Dublin in the State barouche. They were "dressed in white Irish poplin and amused the crowd by the zest with which they responded to any signs of salutation by waving their hands and blowing kisses".[219]

Life at Dublin Castle, the headquarters of the British Government in Ireland, was very irksome at first, as the Aberdeens were never allowed to be alone, and in those days it was still considered necessary for both the Viceroy and his wife to be followed by two detectives wherever they went. But they could take exercise in "a sort of garden at the back of the Castle nicknamed "The Pound". On their first Sunday, having been present at the usual morning services in the Chapel Royal (the official church in Dublin Castle), they intimated their intention to attend afternoon services at Christ Church Cathedral and to go there on foot, the distance being short. They were surprised to find that it was thought necessary to have them preceded by two policemen, two detectives in plain clothes and two ADC's (Aide de Camp) and to have the same number of escorts to follow them.

The "Castle Season", when all the entertainments attached to the regime were held, was supposed to end by St. Patrick's Day, so the Aberdeens had to cram into three weeks the levees, drawing rooms, State dinners, balls and dances usually spread over six weeks.[220]

Lady Aberdeen immediately became President of the Committee formed to organise an Exhibition of Irish Home Industries for the forthcoming International Exhibition in Edinburgh. This was a period of near famine in Ireland with poor harvests and falling prices for agricultural produce. Lady Aberdeen initiated a public meeting with the Lord Mayor at the Mansion House to investigate what could be done to improve matters. One result of this meeting was the formation of the Mansion House Ladies Committee for the Relief of Distress, Lady Aberdeen becoming its patron.

An Irish Industries Garden Party was held at the Viceregal Lodge, today Áras an Uachtaráin, where all the guests were asked to wear garments of Irish manufacture. According to Lady Aberdeen's own account "At first the idea was considered wild and impossible and it was said that no materials were made in Ireland suitable for such an occasion". The answer was to hold an exhibition of such materials on the tennis court at the Viceregal Lodge, where manufacturers were invited to display their goods, and which was attended not only by intending guests, but by milliners and tailors and dressmakers, who were surprised at the selection available. Ultimately, when the company assembled, there was a brave show of Irish linens, laces and embroideries, poplins and woollens; the men were happy in white flannels, or homespun suits and soft hats, instead of the then regulation garden-party attire of frock-coats and tall hats."[221]

The Aberdeens, when they resided in the Viceregal Lodge, held daily family prayers, and a short service on Sunday evenings conducted by ministers of the different Protestant denominations. To provide a setting for these services, a wooden chapel was built by the Aberdeens at their own expense.[222]

During their short stay in Ireland, the Aberdeens visited the south of the country. The description of their journey proves that Lady Aberdeen must have had great stamina. They "stopped for a night at Kenmare, in the midst of beautiful scenery"[223] and where the band had stayed up all night practising "God Save the Queen" to be able to serenade them.[224] During the day they had a very pleasant call at Killarney House, after which Lady Kenmare took them to the convent, where there was a delightful welcome sung by the pupils. The account of the visit includes the information that "at every convent which we visited during our residence in Ireland, there was always some charming manifestation of this kind, organised by the nuns, and although all were distinguished by remarkable skill and delicacy, there was always something distinctive on each occasion. Another feature was the manner in which the nuns invariably kept themselves in the background, leaving the Mother Superior "to do the honours".[225]

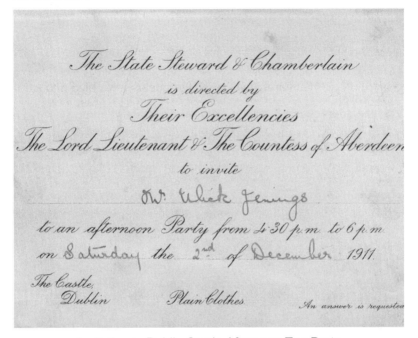

Invitation to Dublin Castle Afternoon Tea Party
(Author's Collection)

The Cork visit was particularly busy. They were received by the Mayor and presented with an address. The following day they received a deputation and an address from the Cork Home Manufacturers' Association; then they visited the Hospital for Women and Children, which was followed by a visit to the School of Art and the Christian Brothers' Schools, where the 800 boys showed how they could cheer. There was a brief recital in Gaelic, offering a "Céad Mile Fáilte". They next visited the Catholic Cathedral, the Good Shepherd Convent and. after luncheon, the Protestant Cathedral, where they were received by the bishop, the dean and various other dignitaries.[226]

Later that day, the party visited Queen's College (now University College, Cork), where they were received by Dr. W. K. Sullivan and the professors. They then visited the excellent Munster Dairy School. Back at the Imperial Hotel they received an address from the members of the Cork Harbour Board and another deputation. This left just time to prepare to receive the guests whom the Aberdeens had invited to dinner. Next morning they set off at 9.30 a.m. to see the Blarney Woollen Mills. Returning by train to Cork, they then inspected the famous Butter Exchange of the city and embarked with a very large party on the steamboat "Citizen" and were taken down the river to Queenstown (now Cobh) for another address from the Town Commissioners. They then took the train back to Dublin but received addresses on the way at Mallow and Maryborough.

During their visit to the south, the Aberdeens visited lace-making centres. Lady Aberdeen saw the necessity for an additional outlet for the produce of the lace schools and, on her return to Dublin, she was instrumental in setting up the Irish Industries Association to manage and market the output of the various producers. The Association's work was divided into two branches; the planning and developing of industries on a commercial basis and the education and training of the workers.[227]

The Association had premises in Dawson Street, later in Suffolk Street and it finally moved to Grafton Street, where Lady Aberdeen negotiated the purchase of the premises of Ben Lindsey, a lace dealer.

Because the Aberdeens' was a political appointment, it terminated on the fall of Gladstone's Government, so they left the Viceregal Lodge and Ireland on 3rd August 1886. For the informal farewell levee, Lady Aberdeen wore a St. Patrick's blue poplin dress trimmed with Limerick lace, and bonnet the same, with rose, shamrock, and thistle. Her early pictures show her to be a striking figure, if somewhat floridly dressed, but in later life she became over-weight and earned the unkind nickname of "blousy Bella". The Aberdeens received a great send-off from the Dublin crowd.[228]

Lady Aberdeen became involved in politics on her return to London, spoke at Liberal Meetings supporting Home Rule for Ireland and Women's Suffrage. In between, the family entertained on enormous and intimate scales at their new London house in Grosvenor Square.

They went on a world tour, including spending time in Canada where they owned land, a fruit farm.

In 1893 Lord Aberdeen became Governor of Canada, an appointment which provided an outlet for Lady Aberdeen's energies. She set up the National Council of Women of Canada and became involved with the Victorian Order of Nurses for Canada, founded in 1898 as a memorial of Queen Victoria's Diamond Jubilee.

Lady Aberdeen came back to Ireland several times during their stay in Canada, presumably at her own expense. The annals of the Mercy Convent in Kinsale record that she visited there in 1893 and made a longer visit the following year. She seemed very interested in the lace-making there and, through her efforts, the school received a large increase in orders, and so were able to keep about 50 girls constantly employed.[229] About this time an outlet for the Irish Industries Association was acquired in London.

Lady Aberdeen's next big undertaking was to formulate plans for an exhibition of Irish goods at the Irish village of the World's Columbian Exhibition held in Chicago in 1893. According to her own account, it proved to be one of the three financial successes of the Exhibition, the other two being the Cairo Street and the Ferris wheel.[230] The Aberdeens were involved in raising the capital to finance the Exhibition and Lord Aberdeen undertook to pay a salary of £500 a year to Mr. Peter White, the secretary. He also provided the salary of Miss Annie O'Brien as office secretary and private secretary to Lady Aberdeen.[231]

In February 1893, Lord and Lady Aberdeen and their little girl Marjorie went to Ireland to make final preparations for the Chicago Fair, making the Castle their headquarters at the special invitation of Lord Houghton, who was then Viceroy.

To quote Lady Aberdeen again:

> The idea of an Irish Village at the Chicago Fair had caught on like wild-fire, and everywhere we went to select the workers we were received with the utmost enthusiasm by people of the most opposite politics - mayors, county people, bishops, and all kinds of folk came to the various meetings, and at Cork the crowd so entirely took the platform by storm when the train

arrived that the members of the Reception Committee were fairly swept off their feet.

Forty girls were selected to work at their crafts at the exhibition. Our only difficulty in regard to the selection of the girls was that the gentlemen of the party always wished to choose the prettiest, without reference to their qualifications in connection with their various industries. Everywhere there were hosts of candidates, but I had to promise the mothers I would guarantee the safety of their daughters and bring them safe back.[232]

The names of some of the chosen girls are listed in the Catalogue of the Chicago Exhibition; Ellen Aher (sic), trained in the Presentation Convent at Youghal, made "the beautiful needle-point lace which was so highly prized by those who were its happy possessors"; Kate Kearney illustrated the making of appliqué lace as it was done in the cottage homes of Carrickmacross and Mary Flynn did the same for the much admired fine crochet work made by the poor women around Clones, County Monaghan, and which was already much appreciated in America. Ellen Murphy made Limerick lace and Bridget McGinley worked her old-fashioned spinning-wheel preparing the wool for Patrick McGinley to weave into the delightful homespuns "whose merits have been found out by the fashionable world, as well as by the sportsman and athlete".[233]

At least one of the girls must have decided that America would provide a better future than Ireland. Maggie Dennehy "who talks real Irish" went to Chicago to demonstrate knitting which was made on Valentia Island, County Kerry. Miss FitzGerald, the daughter of the landlord of most of Valentia, had organised a very successful knitting industry which employed up to eighty girls and women. Tradition on the island is that Maggie Dennehy later emigrated to America joining the ranks of so many Irish émigrés.

The photos reproduced from the Catalogue of the Exhibition give some idea of the cottages where much of the fine lace was made.

On her tour to select the girls who would demonstrate and to inspect the work in progress, Lady Aberdeen visited Limerick where she received an address of welcome, and later met a number of the old and genuine Limerick lace-makers who were then employed by Mrs Vere O'Brien at the Limerick Lace School; one of these said she was eighty-six years of age and was the sole survivor of the four women who worked the bridal veil for Queen Victoria. Apart from visiting those who were to supply material for the Exhibition, Lady Aberdeen went to see Cleeve's flourishing milk factory, and the Limerick Clothing Factory where about nine hundred girls and young lads made uniforms for Government contracts.

The following day, Ash Wednesday, the indefatigable Lady Aberdeen set off for Clonmel, Co. Tipperary, and on to Marlfield about two miles beyond the town. Here she inspected the coloured embroidery produced by the girls of Mrs Bagwell's Marlfield Industry and visited some of the "neat trim cottages". The party then proceeded to Cork. Next day they went to Skibbereen and back to Cork in time for Lady Aberdeen to address a meeting. She spoke so well about the Irish Industries Association and the Chicago Exhibition that Sir John Arnott, the proprietor of the Irish Times newspaper, intimated his intention to subscribe £100 to the capital for the Irish village at the Chicago Exhibition and £1,000 toward the guarantee fund - an announcement which, of course, was received with ringing cheers. Before she left Cork the following Monday, having visited most of the institutions in the city, Lady Aberdeen kissed the Blarney Stone.[234]

The Aberdeens had great difficulty in getting the Irish Village organised. The excellent secretary, Peter White, died suddenly. When a suitable replacement could not be found, his widow undertook to complete the organisation of the fair. Lady Aberdeen considered that the Irish Village would have been a failure had it not been for her.

Connections were used to get people like Cardinal Gibbons and Gordon Selfridge to help. The latter ordered a vest and a wedding veil. He was then a director of Marshal Field of Chicago, before he opened Selfridges in London. He undertook to provide wax figures and glass cases for the Exhibition. We should also give Lady Aberdeen credit for some quick thinking. When she discovered that President Cleveland would not be visiting the Irish Village after the opening of the Fair, she rushed six of the Irish girls (the prettiest ones) to the railway station to give a blackthorn stick and a Limerick Lace handkerchief to the departing President.[235]

The Irish village netted £50,000 for the workers in Ireland and a further sum of £5,000, part of which was used to finance an Irish Depot in Chicago.[236]

Hardship and High Living

The Liberals were returned to power in Britain at the General Election in 1905 and Lord Aberdeen was sent back to Ireland as Viceroy, arriving in February 1906. Again their lives were very busy. Lady Aberdeen writes that "the truth is that from the moment we landed till we left, there seemed to be always so much more to do than we could possibly accomplish in the twenty-four hours, that there was no time for writing journals, and very little for personal letters"[237]

In 1909 the Pageant of Irish Industries organised by Lady Aberdeen had different quadrilles and other dances organised by various leaders to represent shipbuilding, marbles, carpets and curtains, dairy produce, minerals, poultry, milling, tobacco, fruit and flowers, linen, horses, horticulture, fisheries, and Art Industries.[238]

Another of her novel ideas for the time was an open-air Irish play, "Finn and His Companions" by Standish O'Grady, held in the gardens of the Viceregal Lodge.[239]

One of Lady Aberdeen's schemes which gave a great fillip to the Irish lace trade was the Irish Lace Ball at Dublin Castle in 1907. Her Excellency made a condition that those attending should wear Irish lace or crochet as trimmings and, where convenient, she expressed a wish that ladies would wear poplin gowns or have their dresses ornamented with Irish embroideries.

The magazine "The Lady of the House" dated 15th March 1907 gives a glowing description of the clothes worn and a list of some of those present. Presumably, being there, and known to be there, was very important in Irish social life of the time.

Some of the names of the dancers can be identified as belonging to the landed families, like the Countess of Mayo, the Countess of Wicklow, the Massys, the Plunketts and the Villiars-Stuarts. Others had army titles. Both Count de Markievicz and the Countess took part in the eight-handed Munster figure reel, her dress being described as "a lace robe over green chiffon". This was before Countess Markievicz abandoned all connections with the Castle and the British regime.

Another great occasion was the visit of King Edward and Queen Alexandra in 1907, for the opening of the International Exhibition in Dublin. A tour of the West of Ireland was undertaken by the royal group who visited Kylemore Abbey and the remote areas of

Aasleagh (sic) and Glenagimla. According to contemporary accounts, some of the inhabitants thought the King was King Henry the Sixth![240]

Marlfield Workers
(Catalogue of the Chicago World Exhibition 1893. Author's Collection)

A further royal visit by King George and Queen Mary, accompanied by the Prince of Wales and Princess Mary, took place in 1911.

Another of Lady Aberdeen's schemes was the promotion of the handloom weavers in Warrenstown, County Down, who wanted to get protection for their industry when so much linen was being produced in factories. An Act of Parliament was brought in to allow the words "hand-woven" to be introduced in very small letters on the edge of the linen.[241]

Even if Lady Aberdeen had not time to record all of her Irish activities in her diary or to publish them in her book "We Twa", much of what she accomplished is recorded in the Journals of the Women's National Health Association which she founded.

Because she was aware of the miserable housing and health conditions in both rural and urban districts, and the difficulties of subsistence farming, Lady Aberdeen set up the Women's National Health Association of Ireland to educate people in health, the prevention and combat of disease, especially tuberculosis and to help mothers and infants. Branches were set up all over the country and in places as far apart as Pettigo in county Donegal and Valentia Island in County Kerry. By 1910 there were 155 branches. The organisation had its own magazine, "Sláinte", which was edited by Lady Aberdeen. It had reports from its branches as well as numerous articles on the treatment of T.B. abroad. It also had suggestions for improving cleanliness in national schools and railway carriages, general hygiene and simple cooking instructions, including how to budget for food for a family of two parents and five children for 12/6d per week. Improved ventilation in homes and war on dirt and on the fly were recommended, some cartoons being used as illustrations.[242]

Lady Aberdeen described Dublin "with its lamentable lack of houses suitable for the working classes, with 22.9% of its population living in one-room tenements, 12,042 of these families, consisting of 73,973 persons, thus giving an average number of six occupants in each room".[243] One of her first attempts to improve conditions was the provision of playgrounds for city-centre children, where dinners were often provided.

St. Monica's "Babies Club"
(Sláinte. Journal of the Women's National Health Association of
Ireland 1909. Author's Collection)

To combat Dublin's very high infant mortality rate, where 159 out of every 1,000 babies died before they reached the age of one year, Baby Clubs were set up. The idea spread to Belfast, Cork and the towns where the Women's National Health Association was established. The primary purpose of the Clubs was to encourage mothers to use pasteurised milk and classes were provided to instruct mothers in baby care. The Club at Ringsend, which seems to have been the best known, inspired the following lines by a Dublin wit:

So the Babies Club was started in a real Viceregal way
With a feast o' cakes from Scotland and a mighty flood o' tay,
An' Mrs Aberdeen was there in her disinfected best,
An swallowed with her tay as many microbes as the rest.

The ballad ended with the lines

An' then they take the babies from the hampers an' the bags,
An' wrap them up in Union Jacks an' Coronation flags,
An' comb their hair with curry-combs,
An' stuff their ears with silk,
An' give them half-a-teaspoon of disinfected milk.
An' then they dedicate them to the service o' the Crown

An'while they sing "God save the King" they jig them up and down.
They pasteurise them, sterilize them, steep them in the tub,
An' hang them on a line to dry, at the Ringsend Babies Club.

As well as the Baby Clubs, depots for the sale of pasteurised milk were set up at Sitric Road, Arbour Hill, Dublin in the centre of a large colony of artisans' dwellings, situated behind the Royal Barracks and near the northern gate of the Phoenix Park. An American, Nathan Straus, provided the money for the sterilisation plant; the milk was given to the mothers in special bottles, one day's supply at a time, but was only supplied when the dispensary doctor was satisfied that the mother was unable to feed the baby herself. The price of a week's supply of the milk was 1/6d. Other depots were set up in Denzille Lane, at Dr. Ella Webb's Dispensary in Upper Kevin St., and in Dolphin's Barn.[244]

In an attempt to reach a younger audience, the Women's National Health Association started 'Little Mother' Clubs in schools, the first being founded in Cork in 1909. Another movement was the Girls National Guild of Health and the Boys National Health Battalion, both of which were organised on army or scout lines, the girls having "leaders" and "Guild Commanders".[245]

Of all of Lady Aberdeen's schemes, the best remembered all over the country was the Tuberculosis Exhibition Caravan 'Eire' which was bought by the Women's National Health Association with a grant from the Pembroke Irish Charities Fund. The caravan was equipped with diagrams, charts, pictures, literature of various kinds, pathological exhibits, a limelight lantern, with slides for illustrating lectures, and a gramophone.

The staff consisted of Mr. J.O'Connor, a young medical lecturer, who spoke both Irish and English; Miss Manderson, a cookery teacher and demonstrator; Mr. Fitzpatrick, the custodian, who slept in the van, and Cunningham, the driver. In addition to these, Miss Margaret Molloy was in charge of the Tuberculosis Exhibition and acted as advance agent. Miss Blanche Griffin later became the Medical Lecturer. The lantern and the gramophone made such an impression that years later elderly people recalled that the first time they had ever seen moving pictures was when Lady Aberdeen's caravan visited their village.

Chapter Nine: More Irish than the Irish Themselves

The caravan and its staff spent three and a half months in Donegal and Tyrone, where two hundred and fifty lectures were given by the lecturer; about one hundred and fifty cookery demonstrations were given and it was estimated that 74,000 persons attended before the caravan went on fire and was destroyed at Lifford, County Donegal. The Trustees of the Pembroke Charities Fund allowed the Association to purchase, equip and send out a successor, aptly named 'The Phoenix'. The new caravan and its staff continued their good work all over Ireland as the pictures of Rathkeel and Glin show.[246]

War on Consumption Caravan starting on a tour from Vice Regal Lodge Dublin
(Aberdeen Souvenir Album. Author's Collection)

The cookery classes and the health lectures must have brought about some improvement in conditions in the West but they also caused adverse comments. The caravan was supposed to have, for demonstration purposes, slides and cultures of various bacilli and the country people much objected to the importation into their districts, for any purpose, of these things, dead or alive. They were convinced that it was dangerous as "some of the microbes might escape". In

161

Glengarriff it was claimed that the tourist industry was damaged by the emphasis on T. B. in Ireland and that lace sales fell off.[247]

Through the Women's National Health Association, Lady Aberdeen attempted to deal with the scourge of tuberculosis from which, according to official reports, 8,511 died in Ireland in 1908.The Hospitals T.B. Committee was set up with Lady Aberdeen in the Chair and two 'Jubilee' nurses started work in February 1908 to advise on treating patients at home, where the Association provided wooden shelters for the patients to live in isolation away from the family.[248]

Instead of treating T.B. patients in general wards in Workhouses, separate wards were recommended or sheds in the grounds. Accommodation was to be provided for 1,500 patients and several of the Workhouses, including Claremorris and Galway, took up this proposal but not all these beds were occupied, possibly because of the old stigma attached to Workhouses.[249]

Money collected by Lady Aberdeen in America was used to fund the P.F. Collier Dispensary for the Prevention of Consumption in Dublin. In Maryborough a T.B. Annexe was erected in connection with the Infirmary and in Listowel a mansion was purchased at Cahirdown from the Land Commission for the purpose of making it available for a Sanatorium.[250]

The next big undertaking was the conversion of the Isolation Hospital Buildings at Pigeon House Road to a unit for the 'denizens of Dublin' suffering from T.B. of the second or more advanced stage. It was called the Allan A. Ryan Home Hospital because of the generosity of an American, Allan Ryan, who donated £1,000 per year for 5 years.

The official opening was performed by Lady Aberdeen on 23rd August 1910, when she stressed that this was a hospital for the more advanced though not hopeless patients. The Matron was Miss Brennan and the staff included a Night Sister, a Day sister and two probationer Nurses, as well as servants. Electric light had been installed in the building as part of the improvements.[251]

Major Sanatoria were also erected at this period with some help from funds collected by Lady Aberdeen. Streamstown Sanatorium at Heatherside, near Doneraile, in County Cork was the first in Ireland built under a new Act of Parliament, but Lady Aberdeen had some input into its construction because she laid the foundation stone on 14th April 1909. The cost of running the 80-bed Hospital was to be met by putting a penny in the pound on the rates in County Cork. How strong the fear of contagion was can be estimated from the difficulty which the Joint Hospitals Board experienced in seeking a site. Eventually Mr. Creagh, of Stream Hill, Doneraile, placed at their disposal a free gift of 100 acres of Stream Hill Mountain, well away from any centre of population.[252] Later, a large hospital was built at Peamount.

A housing crisis occurred in Dublin when the whole side of a Dublin slum street fell down, killing and maiming some of the inhabitants. A Departmental Committee was appointed to inquire into the incident and, at the request of the Women's National Health Association Professor Geddes, a town planning expert, was engaged to give evidence at the Court of Enquiry. The Professor's Town Planning Exhibition was brought to Dublin in 1911 and all the publicity generated resulted in the formation of the Civics Institute, the Aberdeens becoming joint Presidents.[253]

Exhibitions were a regular part of Lady Aberdeen's activities. She was involved in the International Exhibition organised in Dublin in 1907 and in the Franco-British Exhibition at the White City in London the following year.

Perhaps Lady Aberdeen's biggest triumph was the Ui Breasil Exhibition in Ballsbridge in 1911. The magazine "Sláinte" provided a platform from which to organise. Everybody exhibited at the Exhibition, including the Industrial Schools, one of which had a weaving plant for serges, tweeds and blankets installed at the Exhibition. The boys worked there at shoemaking, carpentry, tailoring, fitting, smithy-work and tin-plate making. All the well-known city firms exhibited and local industries and groups displayed their wares. Entertainments included pony rides, Tofts Amusements, a Bird Circus, Pushball by the 5th Lancers and pipers of the Royal Tyrone 3rd Battalion Enniskillen Fusiliers. A competition for Village Hall Entertainments was won by the Cork Pipers and Dancers. The main purpose of the Exhibition was to publicise Health and Hygiene and all branches of the W.N.H.A. had stalls like "how to clean a House" or "Dangers of fire in the House." Tea gardens and Café Chantants were scattered around the Exhibition and a number of professional concerts took place.

Lady Aberdeen was described at the Exhibition as "charmingly dressed in a pale grey gown of summer fabric, trimmed with lovely Carrickmacross lace; with this she wore a long coat of beautiful black Irish crochet and a large black picture hat trimmed with plumes."[254]

Possibly because of their Scottish background, the Aberdeens were accused of being mean, but in "We Twa" Lady Aberdeen was at pains to point out that they could claim to have entertained a larger number of people and to have given a greater number of dances during their nine Castle Seasons than any of their predecessors. They held a New Year's Day Reception and an annual children's Christmas Party. Lady Aberdeen discounted any suggestion of meanness by quoting that "every year at the end of the season, the girls used to come and say they never had such a good time, yet every year the same old stories about niggardliness started up again. We wish our Comptroller could have seen some result of this supposed tendency in our accounts!" [255]

There must have been some reason for the rumours of meanness if one is to judge from the broadsheet of August 17th 1912 "A parody on Peamount", the sanatorium in Wicklow

> I met a brother Paddy, and shook him by the hand,
> How are you all in Ireland, and how does she stand?
> Said he "The farmers have the ground, and all can wear the green,
> But we've got the curse of Scotland here in Lady Aberdeen".
> Of all the Whigs and Tories that have come to us of yore,
> We never had a skinflint like Lord Aberdeen before.
> He hasn't got the heart to spend a cent or a bawbee,

They split the halfpenny buns in half when Larkin goes to tea.

In their autobiography the Aberdeens stressed that Lord Aberdeen kept clear of all partisanship in politics but, when they supported Home Rule for Ireland, the Unionist landlords and their families absented themselves from the Viceregal court.[256]

At the beginning of their second Irish Viceroyalty, Lady Aberdeen supported Mr. Micks of the Congested Districts Board in his suggestion for the expenditure of a million pounds so that "the scandalous slums of Dublin and other Irish towns could be cleared away, decent housing substituted, and encouragement given to the establishment of industries providing permanent employment." That was also advocated by Dr. Paterson Smyth on the February Sunday in 1906, when he prayed that the new Viceregal regime might see the inauguration of a period of service of the people which would bring in a new era.[257]

According to Lady Aberdeen; "The message accorded with our earnest desire, and we strove to do what we could, believing that along these lines lay the true vocation of a Viceroy in Ireland. But money was scarce, and Ireland was considered a nuisance, and so these matters had to wait."[258]

After the outbreak of World War One, Lady Aberdeen turned her attention to Red Cross work and the provision of a hospital in Dublin Castle for the war wounded.[259]

Their second Irish Viceroyalty ended in 1915 when the Aberdeens were replaced by Lord Wimborne. Lady Aberdeen continued her interest in the Women's National Health Association. The war had already severely affected the financial position of the Association, so the Aberdeens went to the United States to raise funds for it, a mission that occupied them for nearly two years.[260]

From this time onwards Lady Aberdeen had very little involvement in Irish affairs. Her interests switched to the Women's Movement in England and the Continent. She was for 30 years President of the Women's Council of the Scottish Liberal Federation and she was continually involved with the International Council of Women.

Lord Aberdeen died suddenly in 1934; Lady Aberdeen survived for another five years, dying in her eighty third year in 1939.[261]

When we see how much Lady Aberdeen attempted and achieved in Ireland, it is hard to understand why the couple were unpopular, but they were. If we judge by the crowds who came to see them off at the end of their first visit, they must have been popular then with the ordinary people of Dublin. One reason for their unpopularity with the landlords and unionists was their support for Home Rule. Also, their son was suspected of involvement in the theft of the Crown Jewels.

Group of babies fed on milk supplied by Women's National Health
Association's Pasteurised Milk Depot, Dublin
(Sláinte 1909)

Perhaps the best summing-up of Lady Aberdeen's work and
achievements in Ireland was made by Sir Henry Robinson, who was
Secretary to the Local Government Board from 1898 to 1922 and
who crossed swords with Lady Aberdeen on numerous occasions,
and who wrote her obituary. The Aberdeens were, he said:

> An earnest, kindly, well-intentioned couple, but like
> many people who came over to Ireland imbued with a
> desire to show their appreciation and sympathy with
> Irish nationalism, they were more Irish than the Irish
> themselves, a condition of mind when displayed by
> English people, generally amuses rather then impresses
> Irish nationalists. When made Marchioness of Temair,
> one man who should have known better, told me he
> supposed the title of Temair had been taken because
> Lady Aberdeen was such a good fighter, and generally
> carried her way in everything.
>
> Lady Aberdeen's work covered a very wide field; the
> only public health scheme which rather frightened the
> people was the travelling caravan with its lectures on
> the prevention and cure of disease.

Chapter Nine: More Irish than the Irish Themselves

All her other schemes for milk supply, babies clinics, maternity benefit, and children's welfare, generally were excellent. But she had too many irons in the fire, and attempted too much, and in her desire for power, influence, and patronage she interfered with public departments in matters in which she had no responsibility and in a manner which led to much unpleasantness.

She was surrounded with advisers who gave way to her in everything, and never liked the risk of offending her by warning her of financial and administrative dangers in her schemes.

Those who did not yield at once to her proposals were taboo, and I was unfortunate enough to be one of these, and had constant disputes with her; but they never blinded me to the fact of her meritorious efforts for the public health reform, and I never ceased to regret that she was not better advised.[262]

Chapter Ten
Living on the Edge

Donegal Women in the 1890s.

Life on Irish farms one hundred years ago was harsh but the quality of women's lives varied according to the area they lived in and the size of the farms. Large farms in Meath, Tipperary or other prosperous areas had well-built two-storey slated houses and extensive farmyards and outhouses, all totally different from the overpopulated or "congested" areas in the West of Ireland.

Though the Land Commission had been established in 1881, almost all farms were still owned by landlords, who let them to tenant occupiers; the threat of eviction was very real.

Some of the best accounts of life in Donegal are provided by the records of the Congested Districts Board, the body set up in 1891 by the British Government to improve conditions in the over-crowded areas. Before the Board started its work, a survey of the proposed areas was carried out which provides much of the information in this chapter. The digest of the evidence given to the Board's Commission of Inquiry in 1906 and 1907 gives an account of the changes wrought by the Board, including their work for women and is also quoted here.

Unfortunately, the Board's inspectors were all men, who tended to be less interested in the domestic minutiae, so that some details of the women's lives are missing. We must also remember that in rural Ireland in the 1890s there was no running water, no sewage system, no gas or electricity, and that on the western sea-board all cooking was done on a turf-burning open fire, where large iron pots were swung to and fro on a crane.

The evidence of W.L. Micks, one of the Board's inspectors, to the Royal Commission on Local Taxation gives a graphic description of the condition of the people at this time:

> In the congested districts there are two classes mainly, the poor and the destitute. There are hardly any

resident gentry, there are very few traders and officials, but nearly all the inhabitants are either poor or on the verge of poverty … The workhouses and infirmaries in most of the congested districts, owing to the poverty of the people, are necessarily in a worse condition than similar institutions elsewhere in Ireland. Very little is spent on out-door relief. Moreover, there are very few indoor paupers. The people are very helpful to one another. The poor mainly support the destitute.[263]

Secondary sources of income, such as emigrants' remittances and "spalpeen" migrant labour, either in east Donegal or in Scotland picking potatoes, were essential to the maintenance of any small holding. Equally important were the industries: weaving, knitting, sewing, embroidery, kelp-making, sale of sea-weed, sale of turf for firing and donations from relatives in America".[264]

Crochet and lace-making were later promoted by the Congested Districts Board.

Although all these sources were a help to many who could not live on the produce of their small holdings, still, in a good year, some were little more than free from the dread of hunger. In a bad year, arising from complete or partial failure of the produce of their holdings, the result left the people in a condition of semi-starvation.

Who owned the land in Donegal in the 1890s? The three largest Donegal estates referred to in the reports were owned by the notorious Earl of Leitrim, The Marquis Conyngham, (Mountcharles), and the Hill estate. One Mountcharles estate, which was acquired by the Land Commission under the Hogan Act of 1923, consisted of 1616 farms or holdings. The estate comprised 29,191 acres which included a large amount of commonage on the mountains.[265]

What sort of houses did women live in? Women lived on small farms where the families were tenants. Conditions varied according to the relative prosperity of the area but even in the better areas some very bad housing existed.

Probably the worst houses and farms were in the townland of Crolack in the Altnapaste area of Brockagh, where 31 people lived "in the last stages of poverty" and where the inspector considered that nothing would improve matters and that the only solution was to migrate the people.[266] Another extreme was the fishing village of

Inver, which the Inspector considered "one of the most wretched collections of hovels which has ever come under my notice, not fit for pig-sties much less human beings".[267]

Girl waiting to be hired, Gortahork Co. Donegal c.1906
(Bigger Collection, Ulster Museum)

Everywhere almost all the houses were single storey though some had lofts. They were thatched except in one or two areas. The worst houses had only one room while the best had three.

A very poor house in Brockagh is described as "consisting of one room only". The description continues:

> One bed is on the floor and sometimes another raised off the floor, one end of it supported by the end wall of

the house, the other by a block of wood or a dry stone wall about 2 feet 6inches high. The bedding in these houses is of the most wretched and miserable description. At one end of the room is the hearth with a hole in the roof for a chimney, though most of the smoke goes out through the doorway. At the other end, facing the fire-place is the dresser for the bowls, tins etc. The beds are always on that side of the room away from the door. The remaining furniture consists of a short form, two or three stools and perhaps a chair. These houses often have no window.[268]

The Inishowen peninsula in north Donegal was relatively prosperous. Here, "a large proportion of the houses of the tenant-farmers were well placed, well built, and tastefully furnished" but "the poorest lived in low thatched houses where the roofs were secured by ropes of straw or manilla."[269]

In Dunfanaghy district, which included Creeslough, there were many good farms. Here, "the majority of the houses were slated, the slate being procured locally and the houses always water-tight". Inspector Gahan gives a very good account of the interior of these "better" houses.

The interior is not, as a rule, any better than that of houses in other districts, but, with very rare exceptions, the houses have two rooms in them and sometimes three. The floor of the outer room is sometimes paved with slates, and sometimes tramped clay. That of the inner room is often boarded. The furniture consists of three or four chairs or stools and a bench; a dresser for mugs, bowls, teapot etc and perhaps a table hinged to the wall, which can be lifted or let down at pleasure. The bedding is generally plenty, but not clean.[270]

The "Rosses" on the western sea-board was a very over-crowded area but the dwellings were usually well white-washed externally and internally.

Where there are only two rooms in the house the father and mother slept near the fire in the day-room or kitchen and the rest of the family in the other room, the males being in one bed and the females in another. The males got up first in the morning and went out of the room when dressed. In the Rosses cattle in many instances were housed at night at one end of the day-room, and the poultry often perched overhead ... Conditions were improving with separate houses being built for the cattle and fowl.[271]

Probably the best houses were in Clonmany:

The best houses were well-built, slated and comfortably furnished. Windows are large enough to admit light, well glazed, and often neatly painted or whitewashed. In this district I have noticed for the first time, a kind of porch formed within the doorways --- probably as a screen from the violent winds--- and spare bunks, or bed-places in the living room partially boarded up with vertical planks so as to give the idea of a large packing-case placed on end. These are well lined with bedding.[272]

In the first reports to the Board, certain typical family budgets were published, which showed that in some cases the value of the produce of the farm, together with the earnings and receipts of the family from other sources, did not exceed a total of £15 in an entire year; in other cases, the annual resources of an ordinary family were worth nearly as much as £80.

A typical family budget from the Fanad area in the Union of Milford has been chosen to show what income came to the families and how they spent it.

Fanad had a long coastline and average holdings were six acres. The total cash receipts there on a standard farm were £41.12.0. This derived from a variety of sources, for example, the sale of 110 doz hen eggs at 7d per dozen, 20 doz ducks eggs at the same price, 6 geese at 2s each and 15 chickens at 6d. 100 lbs of butter netted £3.6.8.. The stock sold were 2 cows at £6.0.0., 2 pigs at £7.10.0, 3 sheep and lambs at £2.10.0.. 60 stone potatoes only brought in 15s. Much the largest part of the family income, £16, came from "Two harvestings", the money brought home by migrant workers. If the holding was on the shore they might earn an additional £15 from kelp and a further £5 from fish. No contribution by the women from knitting or sewing was recorded.

Rent accounted for £2.10.0. of the total expenditure of £41.12.1. and County Cess, a form of rates, was 7s.1d. Some young stock was purchased at a cost of £4.15.0. Bought food included 7 bags of meal at 12s.6d., bran, 156 lbs of sugar at 21/2d and 39 lbs of tea at an astonishingly high 2s.4d per lb. Other items were paraffin oil, salt, candles and soap; also tobacco, on which £2.12.0. was spent, more than the rent. Passages to and from Scotland or England had to be paid for in cash. The total expenditure on clothes was £2.10.0. for men and £2 for women . Boots were £1.10 and Church dues £1, all totalling £41.12.1.[273]

Interior of Cottage
(Drawing by W. Monk, R.E. from *The Art Journal* April 1907)

The diet all over Donegal was vegetarian, mainly potatoes with whole-meal porridge or bread and in some places Indian meal. The basic diet varied according to the relative prosperity of the families and the area or proximity to the sea. Fish, eggs, a very occasional chicken, milk, butter, cabbage and occasionally bacon were listed as additional items but never all at one time.

In "The Rosses" in winter (15th August to 30th April), the families had "bread, tea, milk and sugar for breakfast at 8 o'clock. Dinner at mid-day consisted of potatoes and salt fish, followed by tea, milk and sugar. Tea at 4 o'clock was again bread, tea, milk and sugar. Supper was at 8, again potatoes and salt fish or bread and tea or oaten meal porridge and milk. In Summer (1st May to 15th August), the mid-day meal changed to Indian meal porridge and milk, also tea and sugar sometimes." This was the period when the potatoes were exhausted and when the women "were killed baking enough bread to feed the family". According to reports, "during the spring and summer eggs and butter were sometimes used at breakfast or dinner, chiefly when the men were engaged in farm work."[274]

In this area the inspector added a comment:

> Notwithstanding the monotony of diet, the health of the people appears to be excellent and the appearance of physical strength among the young and middle-aged men and women is remarkable.[275]

In some areas, including Glencolumbkille, the poorer people had stirabout, made of oatmeal or Indian meal, when they could not afford to buy flour for bread. The bread and the potatoes were cooked in oven-pots on an open fire, no mean undertaking when the amount of potatoes consumed by the family and the stock was given as eight tons per annum.

In almost every report the inspector commented on the large amount of tea drunk and that its consumption was relatively new. It was also stressed that a disproportionate amount of the family income was spent on tea. One inspector, commenting on the Teelin district, which included part of Glencolumbkille, was especially critical, saying that "the quantity of tea consumed is out of all proportion to the means of the people, and the price they pay for it absurd."[276]

Even more critical were the inspector's comments on tea drinking in Glenties:

> Tea is taken universally, and to excess, very nearly at the rate of a pound a week. The description of the tea is black Assam, generally of the worst quality, sold at 2s.8d, or retailed at 9d a quarter. It is on tea that the small traders make their greatest profits, and it is tea principally that the women take in exchange for their eggs or knitting. Sugar is taken to great excess in the tea, about 4 lbs of sugar going to a pound of tea.

The tea is not "drawn" in the ordinary fashion; it is regularly boiled, and is not considered good unless it is almost perfectly black. It is on account of this that numbers of the people suffer from stomach complaints, for the treatment of which, I am told, the dispensary is crowded every dispensary day.[277]

Even in the relatively prosperous areas life was very hard for the women on the land. The northern Inishowen peninsula, which included the town lands of Carndonagh, Ardmalin, Greencastle and Redcastle, had a population of 12,051 in 1891 and of these 390 rural families were in very poor circumstances. Women lived on tiny "farms" or holdings "which averaged about seven acres of cultivated land, 3 acres of oats and barley, 1 1/2 acres of potatoes, 1 1/2 acres of meadow, 3/4 acres of turnips and 1/4 acres of cabbage". Because this area was relatively prosperous, most of the farms had "iron ploughs, a horse, cart, harrow and even a small horse-power threshing machine and a hand-winnower." Because it had an extensive coastline, seaweed was collected and used for manure. In other areas all the digging was done with a spade. Here, women "around the coast also helped materially in the farm work, and their industry indoors, summer and winter, during long hours, is according to all accounts remarkable".[278]

A day in the life of a Fanad family is described by Inspector F.G. Townsend Gahan:

> The home life is very simple. They rise in summer at about seven or later (they are very late risers in Fanad, and one will hardly see smoke at any season of the year before 7 o'clock). The cows are milked and let out and the byres cleaned. Then breakfast. After breakfast work in the fields or digging turf, as the case may be, - the women generally working along with the men. Dinner between one and two o'clock, working then until seven o'clock when, in summer, the cows are taken in and milked.
> After that supper and then to bed. As many of the men go away to Scotland, a great deal of the summer work falls on the women who dig the potatoes and reap the corn.[279]

Townsend Gahan
(History of the Congested Districts Board. W.L. Micks. Eason. 1925)

Over five thousand people lived in the District of Gweedore on very small holdings, only eleven holdings in the 41,314 acres having a Poor Law Valuation over £4 and where 230 families were in very poor circumstances. All cultivation was "by hand"; there were no ploughs. Yet, "the people kept their stock better than in surrounding districts. The cattle were kept cleaner and better and the poultry were better cared for." Here too, eggs were the current coin of the district.[280]

Other work for women on farms was the harvesting of seaweed. Inspector Gahan gave a detailed account.

> Seaweed or "kelp" was harvested for burning and was then sold for conversion to iodine. It was a great source of income to the people but was very hard-earned money. After a storm every man, woman and child in the place is in the water saving the weed, any who have carts, back them into the water, and any who have no carts must creel it up on donkeys, or on their own backs to the grass or sand above high water mark.

This was often women's work, as was the carrying of turf where people were too poor to own any animals.[281]

Seaweed was also harvested for use as fertiliser.

In the inland district of Gartan, near Fanad, flax was still grown though less than previously. This was a very labour-intensive crop and, with the high area of corn grown, as well as potatoes, turnips and cabbage, added to women's work.[282]

The amount of money contributed by women who went to work as migrant labourers either in east Donegal or in Scotland was listed as less than that earned by men, but their total earnings were an important part of the family income.

The hiring of young men and women from Fanad as farm-servants at "Rabbles" or hiring fairs is described by Inspector Gahan.

> Farmers from "the Lagan", the area between Letterkenny, Manorcunningham, Fahan, Strabane and Derry, who wanted help, went "to the "Rabble" at Milford on 23rd May and 23rd November or to Letterkenny on 12th May and 12th November to engage a boy or girl for the half year. Those offering themselves for hire wore a straw tied round their hat or held one in the mouth or hand to show that they were on offer. For the six months work the girls earned £2 to £6 all with keep included.

We may think that the migrant workers were the worst off of all but some girls who were able to make 8s. a week on shirt sewing gave it up and opted to hire themselves out. The importance of the money brought home can be seen from the fact that the "harvestings" of an average family in the Fanad area was given as £16; the next highest amount, £15, came from the kelp making. The sale of two cows only produced £6 out of a total yearly income of £41. 12.0.[283]

Chapter Ten: Living on the Edge

In the Dunfanaghy district, including Creeslough, where there were many good farms, many of the girls still went "to the Lagan" as farm servants. Unfortunately, the inspectors gave no information about the lives of these girls or of those who went to work potato-picking in Scotland.

Women's skills with their hands generated a large part of the family income. In eastern and northern Donegal they worked at shirt making which involved both machine and hand-sewing.

Women spinning and carding wool. Ardara Co. Donegal
(National Museum of Ireland)

In northern Inishowen it was quoted that "sewing by hand or machine in the making of shirts and other light garments is diligently practised in almost every family". The girls trained in a local factory and were then allowed to take the work to their homes. The work was cut out in Londonderry and sent twice weekly to agents in the district who

179

distributed it to the workers. The rates paid were 2s.6d. to 3s. per dozen shirts, the girls earning from 5s to 10s per week. The Singer sewing machines were supplied to the workers at cost price and were paid for by weekly instalments of 1s. 3d. The inspector estimated that the sewing earned not less than £5,000 a year for the women of the area. By hand-sewing (usually making the buttonholes), a girl could earn from 3s to 6s. per week.[284]

The first sewing machines were brought to Derry in 1857 by the Scottish partnership of William Tillie and John Henderson, who set up sewing factories in the area. By the end of the nineteenth century there were 38 shirt factories in Derry and 113 shirt stations supplying them with work, employing an estimated 80,000 strong labour force, of whom 4 in every 5 were women and girls, very often the bread-winners in the family.

In describing Gartan the inspector illustrates the constraints under which the sewing women worked:

> Each girl as she takes her work away from the Depot in Letterkenny has to sign her name in a book and to say what day she will have the work back; if she is not up to the day she is sharply fined. If the work is soiled they are fined also.[285]

Another inspector describes the work in a kitchen in Clonmany:

> Everywhere the hum of the sewing-machine can be heard, and the "white-work" or the brilliant oil-lamp seen at the window of the cabin -- the sound of the machine often accompanying the song of the worker. The machines are driven at high speed; the work must pass the strictest examination; the cleanliness and neatness with which it is done is remarkable. No complaints are made of the ill-effects on the eyes of working by the glaring lamp-light, or from the constant stooping over the machines. Probably the long distances which the workers must walk to receive or return their work, keeps them in health, and the open door of the cabin admits an abundance of air.[286]

Another description comes from Desertegney, near Buncrana:

> The living room, or kitchen, is made to serve all purposes of work-room and store-room, and presents a

busy scene when a sewing machine and needles are employed on "white work", near a window, and the spinning-wheel by the fireside; while the younger members of the family empty sacks of potatoes on the floor, sort them over and prepare sets for planting. Round the walls of such a room will stand sacks of cut turnips, and other special provender for the milk cow or cows. Half the roof space will be roughly ceiled with loose boards, on which the end section of a mattress may be visible; and a bundle of wool fleeces will be secured to the open beams. Occasionally, a sick cow or mare will be accommodated temporarily in the kitchen.[287]

Other accounts of both white work and sprigging describe women working outside at the cottage doors to gain as much daylight as possible.

The other sewing-skill or hand-work was called "sprigging". The inspectors never described exactly what "sprigging" was. Elizabeth Boyle in her book The Irish Flowerers describes the industry as "sprigging" or "flowering", "sewing " or "parcelling" according to the usage of the neighbourhood.[288] The last named title was bestowed because the work arrived to the needlewomen in parcels through the post.

Mr and Mrs Hall, who visited Ireland between 1841 and 1843, quoted the prices paid to flowerers in the Barony of Ards and Castlereagh, presumably similar to prices paid in Donegal.

Between 2,000 and 3,000 girls from 5 to twelve years of age, employed at veining, at weekly wages averaging from 1s.6d. to 2s.6d; sewers employed at needlework for Belfast houses, between 2,000 and 3,000, at weekly wages averaging 3s, about 1,000 employed as needle-workers for Glasgow houses, at weekly wages averaging 4s. Thus upwards of £3,000 was paid weekly in the north of Ireland for the manufacture of needlework.[289]

The work was sent to Scotland where it was bleached. The manufacture at that period was chiefly collars and cuffs.

Hardship and High Living

According to Elizabeth Boyle, a host of factors brought about the decline of the industry; speculation, poor patterns, change in fashion, financial crisis in Glasgow, the competition both of Swiss machine embroidery and of the coarse cut-work known as Madeira work". [290] The Inspectors blamed the introduction of the McKinley tariff which ruined the American market.

Donegal Spriggers at work
(Welch Collection. Ulster Museum)

The work at the time of the Congested Districts Board reports included pocket handkerchiefs and bodices for women's dresses. The designs were stamped on the fabric by the merchants and, accompanied by thread, arrived in a parcel clearly marked with the price payable to the worker. Three classes of workers were employed, sewers, veiners, and openers, families operating in teams. 400-500 Irish agents sent the work to merchants in Scotland.[291]

It had been the main source of women's incomes in Glencolumbkille at one time but had fallen off drastically in the 1880's, mainly because of the introduction of the McKinley Tariff three years previously. By 1892 there was hardly any work at all.[292]

182

Chapter Ten: Living on the Edge

Even more important then, "flowering" was the knitting industry which at this stage was entirely a hand operation in Donegal.

Donegal women were great knitters. Women regularly knit stockings and vests from their own wool for their families but the county was the centre of a major industry as well. In Brockagh District there were 1,412 families in 1891, where sewing both by hand and machine was carried on, but the knitting industry was the main support of the poorest parts of the district where it was a very large and important industry. The principal dealers were Manus McFadden, who employed about 300 families, and Patrick Boyle of Reelan Bridge, who employed a similar number. The rate of wages was very low and the system of payment most objectionable, the work being always paid for in tea, sugar, tobacco etc, never in money, a form of "trucking" or bartering which was common all over Donegal.[293]

All the knitting was by hand in Brockagh district. Yarn was "given out to the women on certain days, generally half a spindle or six lbs at a time. They knit the yarn into stockings, socks or whatever was on order and brought the completed work back and took away more yarn." Four dozen pairs of socks or stockings earned about 6s.6d. Other prices quoted were 1s.4d. to 1s.8d. a dozen for socks and 4s. to 8s. a dozen for long stockings. For special very fine work extra was paid. Gloves were also made in small quantity but there was a great trade in children's underwear, a large order for 200 dozen of children's "combinations" being made for an English firm on one occasion. What really demonstrates the poverty of women's lives is the comment that "often the dealers have to refuse work to the very poorest on account of the dirt of their houses".[294]

The wool used was all imported by the dealers from Alloa in Scotland and Bradford and Halifax in England.

When he summed up women's contribution to the economy of the seven townlands of Brockagh, Inspector Gahan listed 69 sewing by machine, 261 hand sewers, 130 spriggers and 670 knitting families averaging two knitters in each family.[295]

The district of Glenties, which includes Ardara, was the centre of another knitting operation which had started about forty years previously. Messrs McDevitt had the monopoly of the trade and according to Inspector Gahan had made large fortunes at it. Kennedy and Pearson of Ardara, McGeehan and Gallagher of

Glenties and McFadden of Glenswilly between them had an astonishing 3,600 families working for them in May 1892 and Hugh McDevitt, of the original firm, is quoted as being the only one who invariably paid cash for the work done.

Here too, the garments knitted for the trade were mostly socks, stockings and gloves. Most were plain but diamond pattern and other special patterns earned more money. The elaborate patterns took more time to knit and were paid for at the rate of 20s to 40s per dozen for stockings, hard earned money when as many as fourteen and fifteen different threads were employed in the making.[296]

It was taken for granted that women had to walk to and from the agent to collect the yarn and deliver finished knitting, an extra task which varied in each district. Today it seems incredible that girls walked fifteen miles into Glenties because there was no bridge across the Gweebarra River in Lettermacaward. Each girl took with her enough wool for a fortnight, or if they were good workers for a month.

In Glenties, as in so much of Donegal, in most families two or three women worked for the knitting merchants and their united yearly pay amounted to a very fair income. The women were the sole support of their family; the men did little or nothing beyond setting the crop and taking in the harvest.[297]

The other major industry was weaving. The weavers were always men but the women were also contributors because they were the spinners, and carders. To judge from the surviving photos, they were often the older women, perhaps because their eye-sight was no longer good enough for fine sewing.

Glencolumbkille and Teelin were spinning, weaving and carding areas, with a population of 3,125 and 4,827 respectively in 1891.[298] Even though Glencolumbkille was on the sea, the coast was so rugged and precipitous that most of the people led a pastoral and agricultural life. Teelin was the only harbour and was the centre of a fishing industry.[299]

Spinning and its attendant industry, carding, were essentially cottage industries but weaving "was more in the nature of a trade".

Carding and spinning were women's industries. The wool was first carded or combed to clean it from dirt and impurities, a most important process as on the cleanliness of the wool and its freedom from dirt and heather twigs depended the uniformity of the yarn and consequently the quality of the tweed or "flannel".

When carded the wool was rolled into small cylinders about nine inches long and an inch in diameter. The spinner then took one of these rolls and having fixed it to the spindle began spinning. As each roll was finished another was worked in and so on until a large ball was spun, when it was taken away and generally hung up or put in some safe place, until there was enough of them to send away to the weaver, who converted them into tweed or flannel. There were about 410 spinning wheels in the district and 34 weavers.[300] Approximately 17,000 yards of material were woven including check, herring-bone, twill, plain greys and browns.[301]

The best description of the women's clothing comes from the district of Rosguill, neighbouring Fanad:

> The petticoats and vests worn by the women are home-made, and sometimes the dresses of the older women. The dresses of the younger women are almost invariably of bought stuffs, made either by themselves or by the local dressmakers. A dress is made up for from 3s 6d to 5s and 3s for trimmings. Nearly all wear hats or bonnets, which cost from 3s to 7s 6d according to the fancy of the wearer. The men and women are fond of bright colours, red and blue being the favourites. The women generally go barefooted, except when going to market or to chapel, when the boots are carried in the hands until nearing the village or chapel when they are put on and taken off at the same place going home.[302]

Shirt factory, Derry
(Courtesy Cahal Dallat)

Gweedore was another "weaving" area, largely of blankets and underclothing. The people of the district were described as "more energetic in respect of reclamation than their neighbours of adjoining districts and every year fresh lands were reclaimed, not from the bog, but from the rocks. Hundreds of tons of boulders were quarried out of the fields and built into fences or buried deeply in the sub-soil, and the land then cultivated." [303] We are not told which sex did this work but most forms of farm work were done by both.

The area known as "The Rosses" on the western sea-board is described in detail. It had a population of 11,377 but, with the exception of the clergy and doctors, there was only one resident "gentleman" in this district of over sixty-six thousand acres and he was the land-agent for the Marquess Conyngham, who was described as the largest land-owner in west Donegal. The inspector, William L. Micks, commented that the people "lived in such comfort as their means permit" and that he knew of instances where large sums of money had been saved and that many of the men were total abstainers from alcohol. He pointed out that until recent years the fear of an increase in their rent had deterred many tenants from improving their holdings.[304] The setting up of the Land Commission and the Land Courts had given some security of tenure and reasonable rent but it would take time for the results to become general.

At least in the Rosses the young people had a very active social life when they were at home. According to Inspector W.L. Micks:

> They are famed for their love of dancing and they prefer the modern "round" dances to the old country dances. Their dancing assemblies which are held in the winter or early spring, are of three kinds – 'surrees', (clearly a corruption of soirees); meetings for charitable or other 'raffles'; and 'parties' held after a benevolent or friendly labouring assemblage. A 'surree' is a profitable undertaking; it is notified that there will be a 'surree' at a particular house and for each couple (young man and girl) an entrance fee of (say) eighteen pence is charged, the fiddler also being paid often as much as a shilling by each of the young men. The owner of the house keeps the entrance money for himself, and the refreshment (if any) is of the lightest and most harmless description. 'Raffles' for a sheep or some article are often got up by or for those in need of money. The proceedings begin with a dance and terminate with a drawing for the prize. Dancing 'parties' are also given after the gathering of a number of young men for the purpose of digging a friend's land, and in the evening the girls of the neighbourhood drop in for a dance. Drinking of intoxicating liquors is now hardly ever known at social gatherings of any kind, except perhaps occasionally at farewell parties before emigrants leave. On such occasions it is usual for people to sit up at night, and on the departure form what they call a 'convoy' to escort the emigrants for some distance on their way. Apart from these formal gatherings there is an almost nightly practice in the winter called 'kaleying', or the assembling by a few after nightfall at some friend's house to talk and pass the evening without refreshments. During the day "the word goes round" at whose house the meeting is to be, and occasionally the visitors contribute in providing some light refreshment such as tea, and this

arrangement is spoken of as 'a join'. People still assemble in numbers at wakes, but intoxicating drinks are not provided, only tea, tobacco, and snuff being supplied. The clergy are, I understand, in some localities, discouraging the attendance at wakes of any persons except relatives of the deceased. There is not as a rule any dancing at weddings, nor are intoxicating drinks usually supplied. The parents of young couples before their marriage do not, as in other parts of Ireland, "make matches" or get the assistance of professional match-makers. The young men and women, who marry early in life, as a rule, when they meet at some fair or other social gathering, come to an understanding themselves without any benevolent intervention from outsiders.[305]

Inspector Micks considered that the women of the Rosses and Lettermacaward were fully occupied but might earn good wages sooner if they were given technical training early in life.[306]

Teelin was described as the only safe harbour in the area and therefore "the great centre of the fishing industry in the district without which it would go hard with many of the poor families along the sea coast, who, though they all have a little land, are mainly dependent on the sea for their livelihood." The fish were salted by the women and hung up in the chimney to dry or else dried in the sun, but three reasons were given why the fishermen did not use the fish greatly for their own food supply.

Salt, at 31/2d to 4d a stone, was so dear they could not afford to salt very many fish and the people did not care to eat fresh fish. Their houses were so small they did not like crowding them up with a lot of fish. Most telling was the comment that when the price of fish was low the families needed to sell every fish to clear their debt in the shopkeepers' books.[307]

Perhaps life in Teelin could best be summed up by Inspector Gahan's remark that "this teeming population lives always in conditions of poverty and unless for the fishing, many of them could not live at all."[308]

Labourer's hut following eviction, Gweedore c.1880
(Lawrence Collection. National Library of Ireland)

Several women attempted to set up industries to improve conditions in the area. Miss Roberts, an English lady, and Mrs Sinclair of Bonnyglen are quoted in the C.D.B. reports as making efforts to give early technical training .[309] But the largest and most successful undertaking was that of Mrs Alice Hart, wife of a successful London doctor. When Ernest Hart and his wife visited Donegal in the summer of 1883 after a period of bad harvests, they were so struck by the poverty of the region that Alice Hart made a public appeal for money to meet immediate needs and provide seeds for the next harvest. The Donegal Industrial Fund was set up with a capital of £50, to which the Harts added £5,000 and their friends donated a further £1,500. The aim of the fund was to improve the quality of woven and knitted goods and to find a market for them. In 1884 tweeds and friezes were exhibited and sold at the Health Exhibition in London. The following year Alice Hart opened a small shop at 31 New Cavendish Street in London, to sell the Donegal produce. A teacher was appointed to improve the quality of the woven products, especially by promoting the use of better home-made natural dyes. In 1887 Alice Hart was given a Government grant of £1,000 for teaching purposes, which allowed her to put into effect her scheme for opening technical schools for instruction in weaving, dyeing, lace-making and embroidery.[310] Though local women gave great praise to Mrs Hart and the Donegal Industries Fund, the inspector was more sceptical.[311]

All through the reports the inspectors commented on the credit system and on payment in kind or "truck", which was prevalent all over Donegal. The very first report, for North Inishowen, states that "credit is universal and current, payments on account being made from time to time and booked to credit. The interest charged is at the rate of 5% per annum."[312] Here turf and eggs were the principal articles of barter, occasionally hay and corn.[313] In other areas almost everything produced on the holdings was exchanged for goods. In Clonmany eggs were the chief articles of barter; [314] other items mentioned included bogwood exchanged for turnips or other cattle food, load for load in Desertegney, and butter in areas like Gartan.[315] Knitting and sprigging were exchanged in Glenties;[316] sometimes corn in Glencolumbkille[317] and turf in Inver.[318]

A detailed description from Gartan gives a good illustration of how this practice worked:

> In this district as in other districts in Donegal, goods, such as meal, flour, bran, etc., are obtained on credit; but tea, sugar, tobacco, snuff, etc., are almost invariably paid for, generally with eggs or butter, but sometimes in cash; in winter when eggs and butter are scarce even these are obtained on credit, so that in the winter months nearly everything is obtained on credit, while in the summer only meal etc., are so obtained. The length of credit of course varies in different cases, one man may get a year, another eight months, altogether depending on the dealer's knowledge of the customers' circumstances; often when a man is hard pressed, and there is a likelihood of his having some money after a couple of months, dealers will not press him to pay up, but they will charge extra interest on the additional time. Payments are generally made in November when the Scotch earnings come in, and this opens a new credit for them through the winter. Again a small interim payment is made in the spring, with money obtained from the sale of a beast. Through the months of August, September and October, there is no great

amount of goods purchased, so that practically a dealer's credit extends only for nine months.

The extent of credit which a dealer is willing to give varies strictly with the circumstances of his customers, and for some as much as £10 to £13 would be given, while to others it would only be £4 or perhaps not as much, and although the dealer will not press the poor man to pay his £4 at once, still he will not give him any more goods until he has paid at least a portion of what is owing. The interest is much the same as in other districts, and varies from 10 per cent to 15 per cent.[319]

The most extreme terms quoted were in Brockagh where, if a man was so poor that he could not pay, the dealer put cattle to graze on his land, at the rate of 10s for each beast grazed, and 1s.6d. for each sheep. When a man got utterly in arrears, the dealer had often such a hold on his goods that he "sold him out" and stocked the farm for himself. [320]

Inspectors were dubious about the system of trucking. According to Inspector Gahan, "the people keep no account themselves, everything depends on the honesty of the man with whom they deal, and it is in his power to defraud them indefinitely if he choose … It is a mistaken system and the advantages are largely with the dealer".[321]

Further, under the heading "Suggestions as to any possible method for improving the condition of the people" Inspector Gahan added:

One of the greatest pecuniary disadvantages under which the district labours is the system known as the "truck" system, or the "payment in kind system". This system which deprives the knitters of 3d. out of every 1s.6d. they earn, and the farmer's wife out of 1d. on every dozen of eggs or out of 6d. worth sold, is the great strain on this south-west of Donegal, and means a pecuniary loss of many hundreds of pounds to the poor people.

The people cannot object to the system, as if they did the dealers would retaliate by refusing credit, or by increasing their prices. Also the majority of the people are too deep in debt to make any move in the matter.[322]

The fact that one firm, H. McDevitt of Glenties, always paid cash for knitting was so unusual, it merited special mention.[323]

Though women's lives all over County Donegal seem very harsh to us today, they were not as bad as in other areas of the western seaboard. W.L.Micks, one of the Congested Districts Board's inspectors in Donegal, later wrote a history of the Board's work. He considered that "in the County of Donegal alone in the congested districts were there any home industries giving employment to women."[324] He also stressed that poverty was greatest in Counties Mayo and Galway[325] and that Donegal benefited from the fact that the "commercial capacities of the people were well developed."

Chapter Eleven
The Political Prisoner

Cecilia Saunders Gallagher.

The final life in this study takes us up to the early years of the independent twenty-six county State. It is based on the diary of Cecilia Saunders Gallagher when she was a political prisoner in Kilmainham Jail in 1923.

Life in jail, as described by Cecilia was not at all as rigorous as one might have expected. Her diary shows that the women, who were political prisoners, were not locked into cells at any time and had an ordered existence, mainly organised by themselves.

Cecilia Saunders was born in 1889, so she was a mature adult at the time of her imprisonment. She was the daughter of a prosperous middle-class Catholic family in Cork. Her family owned a Nursery and she was one of ten children. Cecilia had been a pupil of Miss Kelly's private school in South Mall, Cork and later at Belrive, the Faithful Companions of Jesus Boarding School in Liverpool, where her cousin Sister Paula Kennedy taught.

After school, in 1911/12, Cecilia spent a year teaching English in a Jewish School in Wiesbaden in Germany. An earlier diary, which is also in Trinity College Library,[326] starts in 1913 and tells of her job in the Provincial Bank where she was paid £2.2.0. per week. Apart from the time spent at work, her days were filled with tennis parties, tea parties, an outing by boat to Curraghbinny, lovely walks in the country, visits to the pictures and card games, including bridge.

When the National Land Bank proposed to open a branch in Cork, Cecilia wrote to the directors offering her services. Her offer was accepted at a commencing salary of £180 per year. She was delighted to leave her present job, as "three years in that place was enough for anyone". The earlier diary shows her interest in all that was happening in Ireland politically, for example, the blowing up of King Street police barracks, the shooting of Divisional Inspector Smith of the Royal Irish Constabulary (the Police Force) and the consequent curfew. The hunger strike and death of Terence MacSweeney in Brixton Jail and his funeral were all recorded.

Cecilia Saunders Gallagher
(Courtesy of her daughter, Anne Gallagher)

Cecilia saw Cork City burning when it was set on fire by the Black and Tans. Her diary showed that she was also interested in events in Europe and commented on the 1914-18 War, showing pro-German sympathies, a common stance among nationalists at the time.

The Saunders were friends of the Gallagher family and Cecilia knew Frank, or "Gally" as she called him, growing up. She was six years his senior but, according to her daughter he seemed to have always been in love with her. His letters to his "ladie faire" are most romantic and many are illustrated with his witty drawings.[327]

Frank Gallagher worked as a journalist, first in Cork, then in Dublin and in London. He became involved in the movement for Irish independence and was appointed to the publicity staff of the Sinn Féin organisation. He canvassed for a Sinn Féin candidate in the 1917 by-election and in the 1918 general election. He also organised the formation of Sinn Féin clubs and volunteer corps throughout the country. He worked under Erskine Childers on the publicity staff of the first Dáil Éireann (1919-1922). On 27th March 1920 Frank Gallagher was arrested in Dublin and spent forty days on hunger strike.

At the end of the War of Independence, when a Treaty was signed giving Twenty Six Counties independence from Britain, the Republican Party were not prepared to accept the Treaty. The result was a very bitter Civil War. Frank Gallagher supported the Republican side.

On 24th May 1922 he married Cecilia Saunders and, after their honeymoon, they went to live in a flat in Dublin. Very shortly afterwards Frank Gallagher was "lifted" and imprisoned by the Free State Government because he had taken the Republican side and, with hundreds of others, he was interned without trial.[328]

Kilmainham Jail was opened for the internment of female prisoners in February 1923. Between then and November 1923 over three hundred women and girls were incarcerated in Kilmainham.

Cecilia Gallagher was among several hundred women imprisoned first in the North Dublin Union and later in Kilmainham Jail during the Civil War. She was arrested on 9th November 1922 and was in Mountjoy Jail until she was transferred on 6th February 1923 to Kilmainham Jail. She remained there until she was again moved on 1st May, this time to the North Dublin Union, the former north city Workhouse near the Broadstone Station, which was partially re-opened to house women prisoners and where conditions seem to have been worse than in Kilmainham Jail.

Cecilia was still in the North Dublin Union when she began her diary on 24th May, 1923. She does not mention being a member of any organisation in her diaries but she may have helped her husband in his activities. Like the other women she was arrested and detained without trial under the terms of the Emergency Powers Act.

Frank Gallagher
(Courtesy of his daughter, Anne Gallagher)

Cecilia began her jail diary on her first wedding anniversary:

24th May, 1923, 10.45 p.m. North Dublin Union.

A year married to-day! This time last year --- and all that has happened since! Our first Christmas spent in jail, both in different wings of Mountjoy and our first anniversary spent in jail -- Frank in Gormanstown Camp and I here at the North Dublin Union.

Cannot write now as I am in a small dormitory with 10 others and there is talking and fidgeting. Beautiful letter and poem from Frank to-day in honour of our anniversary.

Cecilia was transferred from the North Dublin Union to Kilmainham Jail on 17th June and was soon settling in to her new environment.

June 18th, Monday.

A lovely day. It is heavenly to wake up again in a single cell. I am on the top landing and by standing on a stool perched on a table I can see lovely mountains, green fields, houses, people and trams!. This is great after six weeks of nought but church spires and towers, and long waiting queues and large dormitories.

I have a nice cell and have decorated it just like my old cell in A wing. Last Thursday, 14th, six prisoners were removed from the Union- viz Mrs Gordon, Mrs Buckley, Judy Gaughran, Mollie Hyland, Lily McClean, and Eily McGrane. All of these except Mrs G. were members of the Prisoners Council. They were brought here and next day twenty five of us followed them, including Fitz, little Lilly O'Brien, Sheila and Mrs Humphries,[329] Miss Breen, Bridie O'Mullane, Mrs Brown and myself.[330]

The often inexplicable and apparently contradictory motives of the authorities in imprisoning the political prisoners and transferring them from place to place come across in Cecilia's next entry.

June 20th.

We don't understand the meaning of this move at all. We were brought to B wing here and the Governor, Corry, told us that this place was for tried prisoners, and people to be tried, as far as he knew. There were 15 prisoners here from A wing who had been tried, including Fiona Plunkett and Elsie Murphy. These had been here since the preceding Friday, June 8th. It looks as if "the authorities" did this to lower the morale of the girls by breaking up councils and removing Irish teachers and "dangerous" people (like myself). To cloak their move they threw in a few children and harmless people. They are acting like lunatics. For what am I to be tried for instance? When I arrived with Miss Breen of Killarney and Miss Evers, the last three to come, the only cells left were on the basement floor which is very badly lighted but even these were like little havens of rest after the large dormitories at the Union. Anyway, a change in prison routine is always refreshing, and we quite enjoyed the thrill of dashing through the streets in broad daylight in a Crossley tender, with guns all round us! They do things like that to punish and subdue us and we only laugh at the humour of the thing. It is just as well not to dwell for the present on their shamelessness.

XXXX and XXXX protested about our cells on the lower floor and reminded the governor that there was plenty of room in the compound. They advised us not to enter them, as they were so dark, but it was then about 9 p.m. and I decided I would prefer to wait and judge for myself how I liked my cell in the day light. I hankered after the quiet of this place and did not desire the compound with its numerous inhabitants. However, the Governor promised to ring up Portobello (Barracks) in the morning about our admission to A wing and to give us an answer by 2.p.m. The building felt close and had a musty smell, but with habitation and ventilation that has vastly improved since. Next day - either we could all, including the 15 A wingers, return to the compound, or in the event of us 31 deciding not to go, the 15 could go. The latter decided unanimously to depart to their friends, and we decided by a fairly small majority to remain here. The majority of those who voted for going were people who had not previously been in Kilmainham. We had no communication with A wing except by means of a wall separating two yards and on which the A prisoners stand, but we are a happy little family here. The lower landing is now empty as we found plenty of room up here.

Cecilia's diary includes clear descriptions of the daily routine in Kilmainham. She continues her entry for 20th June:

Today I gave a lesson in physical jerks. Programme: Irish 11 to 12 or thereabouts. Exercises 12.15 to 12.45.

Breakfast comes at 8.30 and one needn't get up at all unless one is orderly, but I intend to rise betimes each morning unless I am unduly tired, as I don't want to waste the lovely long day. Dinner 1 o'clock, tea 5 p.m. and a pint of milk thrown in during the day so there is always something for supper, if one wants it. There is no gas in the cells so we each get a good-sized candle which has to do us for two nights. As the days are long, this suffices, with a little bit over for the long nights.

I have received no letters since I came here except five old ones from the Union from May G., Maud, Jenny, Rose and Ursula. Wrote to Frank last Friday and to-day, and home on Monday.

News did filter through from the outside, even if prisoners were deprived of news of their loved ones, as the entry for 21st June shows:

A new bill, the "Public Safety Bill" passed its first reading in the so-called Dail yesterday by - votes to -. It is to cover a period of six months and gives power to the authorities for the continued internment of 'dangerous people' and for the internment of those abusing their liberty by behaviour detrimental to the peace of the 'State'.

Mrs Byrne and Chris Stafford brought from the Union on stretchers. These two complete the 38.

This is Mary Comerford's 20th day on hunger strike. I now understand why I have had no letter from Frank since May 23rd. The Governor informed me today that the civilian censors at Gormanstown have been dismissed and the officers refuse to censor the letters on the grounds that if they do so, civilians will not be re-employed. Woe! Woe! Today has passed cheerfully and quickly but I would love letters from Frank and from home.

But the drought soon ends for Cecilia, with the receipt of a telegram:

June 23rd. Letter fifteenth came, 2 posted, love Gally.

Joy! Joy! caused by telegram as above, so I replied "Wire received, wrote 20th all well Cecilia". So now I feel happy again and await his letters. It is a heavenly day, warm and sunny as I write from my window. There is a baby in the garden below and mother is making it wave up to me. Lucky baby, lucky mother! Ah well! While Frank is a captive I am content to be one too, but it is a day that makes one yearn for liberty. If only we could get out while there is still some summer.

Sheila has called up for a game of rounders so I can't resist and down I fly.

Conditions could be tough for the prisoners, as Cecilia's next entry demonstrates, although the constraints of civil war were affecting the outside world as well.

June 24th, Sunday.

57 girls in A wing started a hunger strike last night at 9 p.m. for the release of one of their number suffering very badly from the effects of a kick given her by a Free State Officer last year. The doctor recommended her immediate release for an operation but they refuse to release her. More savagery!

Mrs Kirwan arrived this morning from the Union. She was caught trying to escape. She had tried to bribe a sentry who played his own game and led her on! Very foolish of her, considering that the same sentry gave promises some weeks ago and had armed police ready at the spot at the appointed hour. I don't know the details of her experience. The poor girls at the Union are still without letters and parcels. Poor little Lilly O'B. I can imagine her going round yearning for letters and cigarettes and newspapers. O'Neill, the governor and his deputy Begley, will long be remembered by any of us who had the misfortune to come under his rule. A pair of curs they are.

The state is surpassing itself in good government! It has now introduced a Whipping Bill to deal with persons caught at "robbery under arms". According to the Public Safety (Emergency Powers) Bill a person may be sentenced to death or to penal servitude for a term of not less than 3 years for armed revolt or for threatening any person or damaging any property in the furtherance of such revolt. With regard to the detention of persons the period is fixed for a week after which he must be released or charged with an offence". Wonder does this mean that they will try to keep the men in for 3 years? Fitz says no, they couldn't do it, they haven't prisons. But they have camps. What is going to happen? There is no doubt but that they are terribly afraid of Republicans, they are so determined to lock them up. However, much can happen between this and Christmas and I think we have only to bide our time and bear things patiently.

The prisoners received support from many high profile Republicans.

June 28th.

Yesterday there was quite a little procession of women up to the gates here to demonstrate re the hunger strikers etc. and to demand our release. Dorothy McArdle[331] was with them, also Mme Mc Bride[332] and Mrs Stuart. Dorothy told us Mary Comerford was released yesterday after 27 days hunger strike. Well done Mary - a great victory and well deserved.

Frank's letter came at last on Tuesday. (26th). He says he wrote on 13th but that letter must be at the Union. He still persists in being optimistic about our release but gives no date this time. I fancy we might be out fairly soon after all for there is a bit of agitation outside about us and talk too in the Dail. As Gavan Duffy[333] said the other day, prison does not change one's convictions, it strengthens them. He is quite right. I have become far more Republican since my arrest than I ever was before. There is great disgust about this new bill "The Public Safety Bill ", especially about the introduction of flogging as a punishment for armed robbery. Once more then, I have become hopeful for release and with that thought, kind friends, I lay me down to rest and sink into slumber. Good night.

P.S. To-day is the first anniversary of the shelling of the Four Courts.[334] I will never forget this time last year. We had only been a fortnight home from the glorious honeymoon and were getting down to ordinary life in our little flat, when the war began. It is all like a dream. Too sleepy to write more.

June 30th. Heard to-night there was a great meeting in the Mansion House re the prisoners. There is to be a labour strike if the untried prisoners are not soon released and there are great hopes outside that we will very soon get out. Perhaps the women will, but what about the men? Meanwhile the Free Staters are holding election meetings all over the country but I see no sign of republican meetings.

Interior of Kilmainham Gaol
(Duchas: The Heritage Service)

News of the release of fellow prisoners was a great source of joy for inmates.

July 12th. Midnight. Fitz was released to-day and three from the N.D.U. on Sat. Why so yerra? I am delighted at these two releases - Fitz's and Lilly's. The former has been ill for some time with a swollen neck gland and has to be operated on. Late last night - nearly 1 a.m. - the deputy came over with the night guard to tell her un-officially, and we all trooped down to neighbouring passages where we indulged in much giggling. For he was decidedly "bevved" and it took on a peculiar form. He was full of good generous impulses but they came at such an unearthly hour! He warned F. not to tell the Governor he had come and that she was to look surprised in the morning when the latter came with her release! This morning at about 11.30 her official release arrived, and there was great rejoicing. Lucky girl, but I suppose she has a bad enough time in front of her.

Am very sleepy. It is ridiculous that one can't get to sleep at a reasonable hour in prison!

July 18th. Mrs Humphries was released yesterday at 8.45 p.m. When the governor came to tell her she was cooking an omelette and she said "It's time for them" and continued cooking! There was great excitement. She and Sheila have been in since November 4th, five days longer then me. I am beginning to get real hopes now but it will be awful getting out before Frank and I'm sure I will. I am in a quandary as to where I should go or what do.

Although generally Cecilia remained remarkably upbeat throughout her incarceration, she, like many prisoners, suffered moments of depression.

July 21st. Saturday midnight. Letter from F. yesterday. Am awfully tired of everything and of jail especially and to-night when I came up to my cell I quite broke down. However I feel much calmer now and at least I can keep away from people if I want to. These moods of depression must come and I think we all find it very hard to be in a place like this while the best of the summer is flashing by outside.

Hardship and High Living

A new prisoner arrived in A wing to-day and we thought they had ceased to arrest women. Had a letter from Leonard yesterday also and one from Hilda[335] the day before. The latter says I am to go straight home and hang the expense. Frank told me that Maud spent all last week getting a room ready for the two of us. Such optimism on Maud's part. I miss F. terribly at times cause there seems to be no one to whom I can turn now.

However, there were opportunities for minor rebellion:

July 22nd, Sunday.

Since last Monday the girls in A wing have had their letters and parcels stopped because some of them wrote things on the floor of which the Governor disapproved. He ordered them to wash them off; they refused and "the consequences were"! I believe the inscription is almost worn off now so perhaps they'll have the letters etc soon.

The limitations of prison life were especially harsh when a prisoner was unlucky enough to fall ill.

July 25th.

One of the girls from A wing has been very bad with epileptic fits for the last two nights. She is in the Hospital and can be heard moaning and choking from the lower landing. It is dreadful to listen to her and how shockingly inhuman to keep her at all when she is like that. Another girl in the wing, Chrissie Stafford, is awfully bad with sciatica and the only treatment she is getting is morphia to deaden the pain. Every night poor Mrs Gordan is up massaging her as the night nurse is of no use. There are lots of things like this that we'll never forget for the State. They are awful and have been awful in their treatment of sick women prisoners. I thank God every day for my health.

Two days later, the epileptic prisoner was released, and Chrissie Stafford followed her out on 30th July. Meanwhile, there were rumours that another prisoner, who had undertaken a hunger strike, had found release in another tragic way.

Chapter Eleven: The Political Prisoner

July 29th. Sunday, 11.30 p.m.

We heard to-night that Nell Ryan was dead.

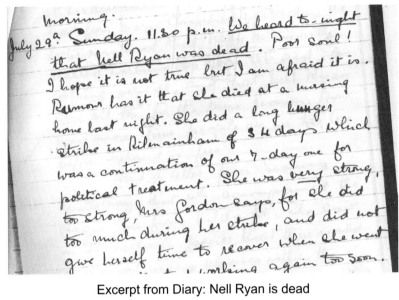

Excerpt from Diary: Nell Ryan is dead

Poor soul! I hope it is not true but I am afraid it is. Rumour has it that she died at a nursing home last night. She did a long hunger strike in Kilmainham of 34 days which was a continuation of our 7 day one for political treatment. She was very strong, too strong, Mrs Gordon says, for she did too much during her strike, and did not give herself time to recover when she went out but started working again too soon. She was a great soul. I remember feeling very sorry when I heard she meant to continue the hunger strike for release. What I knew of her I liked immensely and was glad to have her with us. She was such a fine type and would have been a great help in the organisation of the prisoners. Hence my sorrow as I knew she would be leaving soon. Lots of us were sad because indeed we needed steady people but of course we were charmed at her release. In a letter Sheila H. had from Mary Comerford yesterday the latter mentioned that Mary

MacSweeney[336] started working too soon and was looking very ill, and that Nell Ryan was ill too for the same reason. How many more fine people are we to lose before Ireland is free? Had a letter from Seamus yesterday, that which accompanied the cheque. One from Hilda too. She saw in Thursday's paper that there would be a great many releases within the next few days and they are expecting me home any moment!

I wonder why they are so slow about the releases and why I am now in for nearly nine months. Such rule and such a government! Lately I feel the strain more and am becoming really tired, so if there isn't a move on soon I think I'll burn the prison or do something desperate!

Excerpt from Diary: Nell Ryan lives!

30th, 6pm.

Very mean of Nell Ryan! She did not die after all! Just like Madame Mc B. (Maud Gonne McBride) to let loose a rumour like that from her weekly meeting! Very mean of Nell Ryan indeed to have taken such a great piece of propaganda from us.

In the following days, expectations of imminent release grew among the prisoners. The Free State Justice Minister, Kevin O'Higgins, was quoted as saying that as many prisoners as could be safely released would be in the run up to the General election scheduled for 27th August. Cecilia was hopeful that she and Frank might be included, although Frank's role as a journalist critical of the Government would make him too much of a threat for release. Cecilia later learned that Frank had been moved to A Wing of Mountjoy Jail, lessening his chances of an early release. In the meantime, there were some distractions to be enjoyed.

August 20th, Monday night.

Oh dear! Dear! This dilatoriness is sad for the poor diary! It has been a very bad day and is at present pouring. We were all over in A wing last night at an entertainment. They did three plays for us in great style, Caitlin Ni Houlihan, An Fear Bocht and The Rising of the Moon, and there was a Ceilidh also. We all went in fancy dress from here and we took not only A. wing's breath away with our pageant, but our own also. It was really wonderful and all the costumes were prepared in a day.

We had Brian Boru, St. Patrick, Maeve, Deirdre, Cuchullain, Conor Mac Neasa, Turlough, Strongbow, Mac Murrough, Eva, Owen Roe, Hugh O'Neill, Silken Thomas, (myself), Robert Emmet, Pamela, John Philpot Curran, (Miss Breen), Sarah Curran, Lord Edward Fitzgerald, (Miss Brown), Mangan (Bridie O'Mullane), and everyone you could think of. The costumes were great and were made up out of prison blankets and sheets, brown paper, nighties, petticoats, dressing gowns, frocks and other materials. They were really wonderful. It was about 12.30 when we arrived home and very late when we all got to bed. I made quite a splash with my fairy pyjamas. I tied up the legs and made a frill with them below the knees; I wore a crepe de chine blouse under the coat and had a gorgeous sash made out of a chintz curtain of Miss Browne's. Her dressing gown which is brightly coloured and lined in white silk made a beautiful cloak for me. I turned it inside out and slung it over my shoulder. I made a beautiful ostrich feather from white tissue paper and sewed it on to my black tammy, and put golden buckles on my shoes. It was quite a success. We marched silently into A. wing in our chronological order, while Tessie Doyle (our herald) announced us and our records to the assembled multitude! Mrs Gordon made a wonderful Brian Boru, and Mrs Buckley was splendid as St. Patrick. Miss Burke Dowling (Cuchullain) did any amount of Celtic designs in crayon on the sheets and Mrs G. made a lot of the costumes too."

As the prisoners waited for news of their release prospects (Aodhoghán O'Rahilly had promised he'd work for an amnesty), daily life continued with classes in history, literature and book-keeping. The prisoners lost no opportunity to assert their rights.

August 29th.

The Governor has decided that we are to go indoors now at 8.30 p.m. but we have decided otherwise and we stayed out last night and to-night until 9 o'clock. The adjutant sent a message to-night, that if we didn't come in, we would be locked out, but Mrs Buckley sent a grand reply. We didn't go in and we weren't locked out. Of course all the wild ones, such as Sheila and the kids, were delighted at the prospect of some excitement. But nothing happened!

The authorities caved in to the prisoners' demands and they were allowed to stay out until 9pm and come in at 8.30pm when it got dark at that hour. Cecilia reports another minor rebellion on 11th September:

Racket at A. wing last night and their letters and parcels were stopped to-day. Racket was re the light which is now turned off every night in the compound. The girls made a bonfire and did some other wild things, and it appears the staff came out neither too sober nor too wise and the adjutant fired a few shots. It was all hours when we got to bed. I was up at 8.15.a.m. and had a coldish bath before breakfast, as twas my orderly day.

Sept. 17th. 11 p.m. We have a new Governor and Adjutant who came the day after the racket in A. wing, restored their letters and parcels, and also the light in the compound. Reports concerning him are good.

Exterior of Kilmainham Gaol
(Kilmainham Gaol and Museum)

The release of prisoners continued and numbers dwindled. Cecilia anticipated being moved over to the A Wing where there would be more than 80 prisoners sharing a mere three gas-rings. Meanwhile, Cecilia was dealing with greater responsibilities. She was voted quarter master to the 24 prisoners in her wing. But there were still entertainments.

20th Thursday. Midnight.

Just in bed smoking an Abdullah from a box of them which I won at a Whist Drive in A. wing to-night. Four of us went across - Mrs Buckley, Miss Brown, Mrs Gordon, and myself. Four or five others should have gone but they funked it and we didn't feel like going ourselves but we had promised. However it turned out very enjoyable. They were a nice crowd and it was a cosy room with a grand fire and I wasn't a bit bored. Nora O'Keeffe and Effie Taaffe were amongst the entertainers. The former invited me to stay the night but I told her my feet were cold and that I had to do Irish in the morning! I don't feel sleepy now so when I've read the paper I may be able to do some.

And then, suddenly, it was all over. Cecilia was released on 28th September and returned to Cork, where she described the events surrounding the end of her life in prison:

Friday. September 28th 2.pm.

RELEASED! RELEASED!

CORK. October 10th

This day last year Frank was arrested. So it is now a whole year since I have seen him and how much longer must we wait?

There were 37 of us released from both wings of Kilmainham last Friday week amidst great excitement. Fiona Plunkett and Bridie O'Mullane were the two first to go and half an hour afterwards the Governor came in with a long list and read out our names. I did not feel a bit excited because Frank was still in and I had no home to go to outside, our flat having been let and all belongings packed away in Kilcolman and Sharavogue. Still it was nice being freed at last. Paul Gleeson met me at the gate and we took a tram to Westland Row.

Chapter Eleven: The Political Prisoner

Thence train to Glenageary where I stayed with the Saunders until Wednesday Oct. 3rd. My time was chiefly spent in seeing people and working through the trunks. Sent a wire home and to Frank when I was released. Also p.c. and letter to Frank since but there is as yet no word from him. All communication is stopped with the prisoners in Mountjoy.

Oct. 3rd. Wednesday. Came home and arrived at 10.45 p.m. Met by Hilda, Maud, Fred, Roland and Ivor, and a mob who had come to see if there were any released prisoners. One of the first whom I saw was Mary Comerford. It was terribly amusing the way the crowd surged round me and asked me about their daughters. My family couldn't get near me for some time but finally they rescued me, and I was brought up here to Gallagher's where I am staying at present. Hilda stayed for the night and we saw Mama, May and her children. All looking well but Mama a bit pale. May got fat and the kiddies are sweet.

But though Cecelia was now free; Frank was still facing grave threat. Her diary records the huge anxiety and powerlessness she felt over the next anxious weeks.

Oct. 21st.

Frank is on hunger-strike for unconditional release, with about 440 other men in Mountjoy. The strike began this day last week so that he has now completed eight days. Yesterday I completed a Novena of Holy Communions for F's release. I started it before I knew of the hunger strike and I do hope the Lord will hear my prayers. Dear Lord do!

Oct. 31st. Wednesday.

Frank's 18th day of hunger strike. Nov. 17th. Saturday. 35th day of hunger strike. F. must be very weak now. I write every day and have sent F. books, eau-de-cologne etc. and he writes every week. Oh dear! Oh dear! This country is never worth it."

Frank survived the hunger strike and was eventually released from prison.

According to Anne, the couple's adopted daughter, life was difficult for them following their release from prison, and they travelled extensively on the Continent for the next few years. From the late 1920's until 1931 they lived in Raheny House, now the Garda Retirement Home. They eventually settled in Sutton with their two adopted daughters, first at Bellvue House and later at "Glor na Mara". Cecilia did much work for the local Red Cross during the "Emergency" of World War II. Frank Gallagher returned to journalism and to writing. He got a massive stroke in 1955 and was looked after at home by Cecilia until his death in 1962. She died five years later. Her daughter Anne writes that "she was a very remarkable woman and was loved by all who knew her".

References

Chapter One

[1] This information is drawn from *The Hopeful Traveller, The Life and Times of Daniel Augustus Beaufort*, by Canon C. Ellison, Boethius Press, Kilkenny, 1987.

[2] Mary Beaufort's eldest surviving daughter, Frances Anne, was Richard Lovell Edgeworth's fourth wife and the mother of six of his children. She was therefore the step-mother of the novelist, Maria Edgeworth.

[3] The wife of the bishop, and cousin of Mary Beaufort.

Chapter Two

[4] *Selina Crampton's Diary for 1817*, in Trinity College, Dublin, Ref. No. 4197.

[5] *Dictionary of National Biography, Volume 5, Oxford University Press, London, reprinted in 1973*

[6] *Bicentenary Account of the Royal College of Surgeons in Ireland 1784-1984*, Vol. 2, p.416.

[7] *Marriages in St. Peter's Parish Church, Dublin, for the year 1817.* Book 3, p. 215.

[8] Cameron, Sir Charles, *History of the Royal College of Surgeons in Ireland and of Irish Schools of Medicine*, Fannin and Co, Dublin, 1916.

[9] Thoms Directories for 1833 and 1838 show Philip Crampton residing at No. 15 Merrion Square North, but it appears that Merrion Square has been renumbered more than once.

[10] ibid.

[11] *Index to Dublin Wills 1770-1800, Appendix to 26th Report.*

[12] Coakley, D., *The Irish School of Medicine. Outstanding practitioners of the nineteenth century*, Town House, Dublin, 1988, p. 89.

[13] *Gentlemens and Citizens Almanack*, compiled by John Watson Stewart for the year 1817.

[14] Mooney, Ed, Byrne, Peter, *New History of Ireland*, TCD, Dublin 1996, p??

[15] Information from the Archives of the Adelaide Hospital, Dublin.

[16] Feinaiglian Institution set up in 1813 by Professor Feinaigle van Luxembourg at Aldborough House using a system of education he devised.

[17] Lady Landaff lived at Number 6, Merrion Square South.

[18] Later renamed O'Connell Bridge

Chapter Three

[19] Letters from Maria Edgeworth, Ballytore Papers, MS 989, National Library of Ireland, Kildare Street, Dublin.

[20] An order dated March 1847 to discontinue work and roads drainage work.

Chapter Four

[21] From a paper entitled "State-aided emigration schemes from Crown Estates in Ireland c. 1850", by Eilish Ellis M.A. Compiled from the Quit Rent Office Collection of books and papers transferred to the Public Record Office Dublin in 1943 and now in the National Archives. Permission to quote from the paper has been given by Mrs Ellis.

Chapter Five

[22] The information in this chapter has been largely drawn from the M. Ed. Thesis of historian Anne Lanigan, who has kindly permitted me to use her research into the actual records of seven of the nine County Tipperary Workhouses for the years 1840-1880. These records provide a surprisingly open and unvarnished account of life within the institutions, consisting of comments, orders and letters from a wide variety of sources – assorted officers of the house, Poor

Law and National Education inspectors, chaplains, sundry visitors, and Visiting Committees of the Board of Guardians. Accounts from inmates and nursing staff in other Unions are also included.

[23] Beales, Derek, *From Castlereagh to Gladstone*, London: Nelson 1969, p. 42.

[24] *Fifth Annual Report of the Poor Law Commissioners*, 1839, p. 24.

[25] *op. cit*, p. 33.

[26] *ibid*, p. 27.

[27] *ibid*, p. 82.

[28] *Report of Commission for Inquiring into the Execution of Contracts for Certain Union Workhouses in Ireland*, House of Commons, 1844, Vol. XXX, p. 83.

[29] Burke, Helen, *The People and the Poor Law*, Dublin: Women's Education Bureau, 1987, p. 44.

[30] Nicholson, Asenath, *Annals of the Famine in Ireland*, Dublin: Lilliput Press reprint 1998, p. 109.

[31] Fifth Annual Report, PLC, 1839, Appendix A, No. 9, plan p. 80.

[32] Sixth Annual Report, PLC, 1840, p. 71.

[33] Cashel Minute Book No. 23, p. 92.

[34] Cashel M.B. No. 45, p. 273; Clonmel M.B. No. 37, p. 1010.

[35] Thurles M.B. No. 1, p. 117

[36] Thurles M.B. No. 75, p. 441.

[37] Seventh Annual Report, PLC, 1841, p. 121.

[38] Eighth Annual Report PLC, 1842, p. 106.

[39] Seventh Annual Report PLC, 1841, p. 123.

[40] ibid, p. 123

[41] Third Annual Report PLC, check date, p. 81.

[42] Roscrea M.B. No. 14, 30th January, 1852; Tipperary M.B. No. 12, p. 152.

[43] Sixth Annual Report, PLC, 1840, p. 237

[44] ibid

[45]ibid, p. 328

[46] Asenath Nicholson, p. 109.

[47] Eighth Annual Report, Local Government Board, 1880, Appendix A No. 2, p. 10

[48] Seventh Annual Report PLC, 1841, p. 125

[49] "The Workhouse Problem," *New Ireland Review* Vol XVI (September 1900), p. 29.

I.First Annual Report, Irish Poor Law Commission, 1848, p. 171.

[51] *Parliamentary Gazetteer of Ireland*, Dublin: Fullerton & Co 1846, Vol. 3, p. 343.

[52] Thurles M.B. No. 20, p. 82.

[53] Thirteenth Annual Report PLC, 1847, p. 209.

[54] ibid.

[55] Clonmel M.B. No. 2, p. 184 and No. 6, p. 265.

[56] Third Annual Report, IPLC, 1850, p. 56.

[57] Thurles M.B. No 17, p. 211.

[58] Carlyle, Thomas, *Reminiscences of my Irish Journey in 1849*, London: Sampson Low, 1882, p. 82.

[59] Ward, Patrick Roe, "In an Ulster Workhouse", *The Bell* Vol. XV, No. 4 (January 1948), p. 27.

[60] Tipperary M.B., No. 1, p. 43.

[61] Clonmel M.B. No. 1, p. 392; Nenagh M.B. No. 8, p. 418.

[62] Tenth Annual Report PLC, 1844, p. 341.

[63] Ward, Patrick Roe, op.cit, p. 28.

[64] Tenth Annual Report PLC, 1844, p. 331.

[65] ibid, p. 328.

[66] Clonmel M.B. No. 37, p. 110.

[67] Roscrea M.B. No. 1, p. 33

[68] Tipperary M.B. No. 3, p. 518

[69] Tipperary M.B. No. 2, p. 147

[70] Thurles M.B. No. 38, p. 188.

[71] ibid, M.B. No. 33, p. 43.

[72] Dyos Wolff, eds, *The Victorian City: Images and Realities*, two volumes, London: Routledge & Keegan Paul, 1973, Vol. 2, p. 403.

[73] Nenagh M.B. No. 37, & January, 1871.

[74] Tipperary M.B. No. 9, 29th May 1849; Roscrea M.B. No. 3, p. 237.

[75] Roscrea M.B. No. 32, 12th April 1877.

[76] Cashel M.B. No. 28, p. 327.

[77] Nenagh M.B. No. 23, p. 249; Thurles M.B. No. 21, p. 20.

[78] Nenagh M.B. No. 43, p. 115

[79] Nenagh M.B. No. 40, p. 140.

[80] Cashel M.B. No. 65, p. 207; Clonmel M.B. No. 63, p. 50; Thurles M.B. No. 75, p. 343; Cashel M.B. No. 65, p. 207.

[81] Clonmel M.B. No.41, p. 289.

[82] Burke, op.cit, p. 193-4.

[83] Roscrea M.B. No. 19, 15th September, 1855.

[84] Clogheen M.B. No. 52, p. 178.

[85] Cashel M.B. No. 8, p. 148.

[86] Nenagh M.B. No. 40, pp. 90, 150, 170.

[87] Roscrea M.B. No. 15, 30th July 1852.

[88] Cashel M.B. No. 30, p. 38.

[89] Tipperary M.B. No. 23, p. 103; M.B. No. 24, p. 884; M.B. No. 25, p. 503.

[90] Roscrea M.B. No. 46, 20th May 1880; Thurles M.B. No. 34, p. 155.

[91] Clonmel M.B. No. 46, p. 452.

[92] Thurles M.B. No. 58, p. 439; M.B. No. 59, p. 423.

[93] Cashel M.B. No. 34, p. 145.

[94] Burke, op.cit., p. 223.

[95] ibid, p. 209.

[96] ibid, p. 213-214.

[97] Clogheen M.B. No. 48, p. 49.

[98] Roscrea M.B. No. 8, p. 385; Cashel M.B. No. 14, p. 87.

[99] Thurles M.B. No. 16, p. 109.

[100] Thurles M.B. No. 58, p. 439; Cashel M.B. No. 34, p. 145.

[101] Robins, Joseph, *The Lost Children*, Dublin: Institute of Publication Administration, 1980, pp. 236-7.

[102] Tipperary M.B. No. 16, p. 330.

[103] Cashel M.B. No. 17, p. 417.

[104] Roscrea M.B. No. 43, 29th March, 1877; Nenagh M.B. No. 43, p. 55; Nenagh M.B. No. 45, p. 64; Cashel M.B. No. 42, p. 134.

[105] Twentieth Annual Report, Commission of National Education, 1853, p. 654.

[106] Roscrea M.B. No. 46, p. 27. May 1880.

[107] Thurles M.B. No. 11, p. 132.

[108] Tipperary M.B. No. 40, p. 633.

[109] Roscrea M.B. No. 329, 2 June 1863.

[110] Nenagh M.B. No. 43, p. 97.

[111] Thurles M.B. No. 29, p. 182.

[112] Cashel M.B. No. 25, p. 251; M.B. No. 42, p. 203; M.B. No. 50, p. 139, 353.

[113] Thurles M.B. No. 20, p. 88; M.B. No. 23, p. 90; M.B. No. 24, p. 27; M.B. No. 25, p. 22; M.B. No. 26, p. 30; M.B. No. 33, p. 157.

[114] Information from Sister Teresa, Sisters of Mercy, Western Province Archives, Galway.

[115] Information from Sister Veronica Crowley, Poor Servants of the Mother of God Convent, Chapelizod, Dublin.

Chapter Six

[116] Quoted in Livingstone, Peadar, *The Fermanagh Story*, p. 204.

[117] Catalogue of the Dublin International Exhibition of 1865, p. 273.

[118] *The Limerick Chronicle*, 4th November, 1843.

[119] Undated hand-written account from Mrs Florence Vere O'Brien's private papers.

[120] ibid.

[121] ibid.

[122] Information supplied by the Good Shepherd Convent, December 1984.

[123] Information supplied by Veronica Rowe, grand-daughter of Mrs Vere O'Brien.

[124] ibid.

[125] Information supplied by Sister Imelda of the Mercy Convent, Kinsale, in October 1983.

[126] ibid.

[127] Catalogue of the Colombian Exhibition, Chicago 1893.

[128] Information to author from annals of the Ursuline Convent, Cork.

[129] Meredith, Louisa Ann, *The Lacemakers: sketches of Irish character. Efforts to establish lacemaking in Ireland*. London: Jackson, Walford and Hodder, 27 Paternoster Row. 1865,p.56

[130] op.cit, p.56.

[131] ibid.

[132] ibid.

[133] op.cit, p.213 onwards

[134] ibid.

[135] ibid.

[136] ibid.

[137] ibid.

[138] ibid.

[139] ibid.

[140] Micks, W.L., *History of the Congested Districts Boards*, Dublin: Easons, 1925, p. 70.

[141] Index to Evidence 1908 to Royal Commission on Congestion in Ireland, p. 176.

[142] Micks, op.cit, p. 67

[143] Index to Evidence, p. 176.

[144] Index to Evidence, p. 549.

[145] ibid, p. 176.

[146] Micks, op. cit, p. 70.

[147] Index to Evidence, p. 79.

[148] Index to Evidence., p. 176.

[149] ibid, p. 535.

[150] ibid, p. 176.

[151] Micks, op. cit, , p. 77.

Chapter Seven

[152] Woodham Smith, Cecil, Florence Nightingale, London: Constable, 1950, p. 134.

[153] op.cit., p. 135.

[154] ibid, p. 135.

[155] ibid, p. 139.

[156] ibid, p. 143.

[157] ibid, p. 146.

[158] Sister Aloysius, *Memories of the Crimea*, London: Burns and Oates, 1897, p. 7.

[159] In Memoriam card lent by Sister M. de Lourdes, Mercy Convent, Gort.

[160] Concannon, Senator Helena, "The Sisters of Mercy in the Crimean War", pamphlet, Irish Messenger Office, 5 Great Denmark Street, Dublin, 27th November, 1950.

[161] Bolster, Angela, *The Sisters of Mercy in the Crimean War*, Cork: Mercier Press, 1964, p. 143.

[162] Undated article by Sister M. de Lourdes, Mercy Convent, Gort.

[163] Sr. Aloysius, p. 18.

[164] ibid,, p. 16.

[165] ibid, p. 17

[166] ibid, p. 21.

[167] ibid, p. 21.

[168] ibid, p. 23.

[169] Bolster, p. 72.

[170] ibid, p. 73.

[171] ibid, p. 73.

[172] ibid, p. 74.

[173] ibid, p. 75.

[174] ibid, p. 75.

[175] ibid, p. 79.

[176] Woodham Smith, p. 232.

[177] Bolster, p. 97.

[178] ibid,, p. 97.

[179] Sister Aloysius, p. 33.

[180] ibid,, p. 34.

[181] ibid, p. 36.

[182] ibid, p. 36.

[183] ibid, p. 37.

[184] ibid, p. 39.

[185] ibid, p.40.

[186] ibid, p. 41.

[187] ibid, p. 41.

[188] ibid, p. 42.

[189] ibid, p. 43.

[190] Bolster, p. 121.

[191] Sister Aloysius, p. 49.

[192] ibid, p. 49.

[193] Bolster, p. 151.

[194] Sister Aloysius, p. 49.

[195] ibid, p. 54.

[196] ibid, p. 55.

[197] ibid, p. 57.

[198] ibid, p. 62.

[199] ibid, p. 63.

[200] ibid, p. 66.

[201] ibid, p. 66.

[202] ibid, p. 67.

[203] ibid, p. 70.

[204] ibid, p. 71.

[205] ibid, p. 71.

[206] Bolster, p. 230.

[207] Sister Aloysius, p. 76.

[208] ibid, p. 76.

[209] Bolster, p. 214.

[210] Sister Aloysius, p. 94.

[211] Bolster, p. 148.

[212] Sister Aloysius, p. 95.

[213] Information from Sister M. de Lourdes Fahy, Convent of Mercy, Gort and Mercy Convent Archives, Baggot Street, Dublin.

[214] Woodham Smith, p. 229.

[215] ibid, p. 232.

Chapter Eight

[216] Hedderman, B.M, *Glimpses of My Life on Aran,*, Bristol: John Wright and Sons, 1917.

Chapter Nine

[217] *We Twa*. Reminiscences of Lord and Lady Aberdeen. Vols I and II. Published by W. Collins, Sons and Co. Ltd, London, Sydney and Auckland. 1925, p. 89, Vol I.

[218] *We Twa*, Vol I., p. 187.

[219] op.cit, Vol I, p. 252.

[220] ibid, Vol I, p. 253.

[221] Lady Aberdeen, *The Musings of a Scottish granny*, Heath Cranton, London 1936. 1936, p. 135

[222] *We Twa*, Vol I., pp. 257-8.

[223] op.cit, Vol I, p. 259.

[224] ibid, Vol I, p. 260.

[225] ibid, Vol I, p. 261.

[226] ibid, Vol I, p. 262.

[227] *The Musings of a Scottish granny*, p. 137.

[228] *We Twa*, Vol. I, p. 266.

[229] Annals, Mercy Convent, Kinsale, Co. Cork.

[230] *The Musings of a Scottish granny*, p. 139.

[231] op.cit, p. 140.

[232] *We Twa*, Vol. I., p. 326.

[233] *The Musings of a Scottish granny*, p. 143.

[234] Catalogue of the Columbian Exhibition, Chicago 1893.

[235] *We Twa*, Vol. II, p. 176.

[236] Souvenir album presented to the Aberdeens, undated.

[237] *Slainte, Journal of the Women's National Health Association*, Edited by Lady Aberdeen, 1911.

[238] *We Twa*, Vol. II, p. 182.

[239] op.cit, Vol. II, p. 183.

[240] Robinson, Right Hon. Sir Henry, *Memories wise and otherwise*, London, New York, Toronto and Melbourne: Cassell and Co. Ltd, 1923, p. 152.

[241] *Slainte*, 1911.

[242] *Slainte*, 1909/10/11.

[243] *We Twa*, Vol. II, p. 187.

[244] *Slainte*, 1909.

[245] *Slainte*, 1910.

[246] *Slainte*, 1909.

[247] *Slainte*, 1909/1910.

[248] *Slainte*, 1910.

[249] *Slainte*, 1910.

[250] *Slainte*, 1910.

[251] *Slainte*, 1910.

[252] *Slainte*, 1911.

[253] *We Twa* Vol. II, p. 188.

[254] *Slainte*, 1911.

[255] *We Twa* Vol. II, p. 179.

[256] *We Twa*, Vol. II, p. 179.

[257] op.cit, p. 186.

[258] op.cit, p. 186.

[259] op.cit, Chapter XVI, p. 224 onwards

[260] op.cit, Chapter XIX, p. 276.

[261] Obituary. *Manchester Guardian*. 19th April 1939.

[262] Robinson, p. 224-227.

Chapter Ten

[263] *Evidence incorporated in the Special Report presented by Lord Balfour of Burleigh and Lord Blair Balfour. Ireland industrial and agricultural.* Dublin: Browne and Nolan and Co, 1902, p. 260.

[264] Micks, W.L., History of the Congested Districts Board, Dublin: Eason and Co, 1925, p. 9.

[265] Land Commission Index of Estates.

[266] Congested Districts Boards Inspectors Base Line reports, referred to as C.D.B. reports. Compiled and printed 1892-94. Dublin: Alex Thom and Co, the Queen's Printing Office, 87089 Abbey Street, p. 89.

[267] op.cit, p. 222.

[268] ibid, p. 87.

[269] ibid, p. 17.

[270] ibid, p. 99.

[271] ibid, p. 135.

[272] ibid, p. 27.

[273] ibid, p. 46.

[274] ibid, p. 133.

[275] ibid, p. 133.

[276] ibid, p. 193.

[277] ibid, p. 163.

[278] ibid, p. 9.

[279] ibid, p. 48.

[280] ibid, p. 118.

[281] ibid, p. 42, 43.

[282] ibid, p. 65.

[283] ibid, p. 42.

[284] ibid, p. 12.

[285] ibid, p. 69.

[286] ibid, p. 27.

[287] ibid, p. 34.

[288] Boyle, Elizabeth, *The Irish Flowerers*, Belfast: Ulster Folk Museum and Institute of Irish Studies, Queen's University, 1971, p. 22.

[289] *Hall's Ireland: its scenery and character*, Vol. III, 1841-43, Virtue & Company, London, 1842

[290] Boyle, p. 70.

[291] op.cit, p. 70.

[292] C.D.B. Inspectors Base Line Reports, p. 185.

[293] op.cit, p. 81.

[294] ibid, p. 82.

[295] ibid, p. 82.

[296] ibid, p. 155-56.

[297] ibid, p. 127.

[298] ibid, p. 167 and 179.

[299] ibid, p. 187.

[300] ibid, p. 174.

[301] ibid, pp. 172-3.

[302] ibid, p. 61.

[303] ibid, p. 118.

[304] ibid, p. 134.

[305] ibid, p. 135.

[306] ibid, p. 138.

[307] ibid, p. 188.

[308] ibid, p. 195.

[309] ibid, p. 138.

[310] Boyle, p. 75

[311] C.D.B. inspectors base line reports, p. 121.

[312] op.cit, p. 16.

[313] ibid, p. 16

[314] ibid, p. 26.

[315] ibid, p. 33.

[316] ibid, p. 162.

[317] ibid, p. 176.

[318] ibid, p. 218.

[319] ibid, p. 70.

[320] ibid, p. 84.

[321] ibid, p. 59.

[322] ibid, p. 89.

[323] ibid, p. 156 and *History of the Congested Districts Board*, p. 82.

[324] *History of the Congested Districts Board*, p. 67.

[325] op.cit, p. 67.

Chapter Eleven

[326] Information supplied by Anne Gallagher, Cecilia's adopted daughter.

[327] From the Gallagher Papers, Trinity College Dublin, Ref. No. 10050-10055

[328] op.cit.

[329] The niece and sister of The O'Rahilly, who was executed in 1916.

[330] Sheila Humphries became the leader and chief organiser of the group of women prisoners.

[331] Historian and later author of *The Irish Republic*

[332] Maud Gonne McBride, widow of John McBride, executed signatory of the Proclamation on Easter Monday, and beloved of William Butler Yeats.

[333] George Gavan Duffy, signatory of the Treaty and a member of the Free State Government

[334] This event was the first act in the Civil War.

[335] Ceclia's sister.

[336] Sister of Terence MacSweeney, Lord Mayor of Cork, who died on hunger-strike in Brixton Prison.